AF808532

Letters From Babylon

a story of

EXILE

and

RETURN

Camilla Smith

Letters From Babylon: *A Story of Exile and Return*

Grateful acknowledgment is made for permission from

James Hollis to quote from his works.

The works of Rainer Maria Rilke and Rabindranath Tagore are in the public domain.

All scripture was taken from the King James version of the Bible.

COVER DESIGN: Linda King

Contact publisher for more information: fauxpoets@gmail.com

ISBN: 978-0-578-46986-7 (Faux Poets Press)

Proudly printed in the United States of America.

Faux Poets Press, PO Box 664 Mayfield, KY 42066

CONTENTS

DEDICATION

This book is dedicated to the memory of all those who, because of their love for God, took risks, made sacrifices and faced the unknown, and by so doing gave me and many others a better life.

Home...what a nice word. The word brings up memories of happier times. But what if home becomes toxic, or ceases to exist? What if one finds oneself an exile in a strange land? There are many reasons to undertake this dark journey. Soldiers who leave the camaraderie and structure of the military can find themselves struggling to recreate themselves in a civilian world. An addict or an alcoholic may love the world he comes from but know that he can never return. People who come from abuse or dysfunction may find themselves outside of their culture and comfort zone, sometimes through circumstances, and sometimes through their own choice. All these possibilities present the challenge of learning to live—not only to live but to sing—in a strange land. It should be our goal to come through this wilderness of angst, pain and despair with a new perspective and the capacity to not only survive, but to thrive. My own personal journey is not any of those named above, but the story provides a backdrop for surviving exile...finding meaning and a song in a strange land. And if we can learn to sing again, maybe we can help others who are struggling with such great and painful difficulties. We are all a family and we all need one another!

By the rivers of Babylon, there we sat down, yea, we wept, when we remembered Zion.
We hanged our harps upon the willows in the midst thereof, for there they that carried us away captive required of us a song; and they that wasted us required of us mirth, saying, Sing us one of the songs of Zion.
How shall we sing the LORD'S song in a strange land?
If I forget thee O Jerusalem, let my right hand forget her cunning.

-Psalm 137:1-5

We are asked to bear what is often felt to be unbearable. This is the task awaiting us in the swampland of the soul we call loneliness—to bear the unbearable. But in so doing, by "going through," one breaks the hold of the primal fear that holds sway over much of our lives. To go through it with the insight and courage of an adult, to make friends with it, somehow breaks that tyrannous hold.[1]

-James Hollis, Swamplands of the Soul

---

[1] Swamplands of the Soul, p 64

Home

The message of loss and grief and betrayal is that we cannot hold on to anything, cannot take anything or anyone for granted, cannot spare ourselves acute pain. But what abides is the invitation to consciousness. What is constant amid inconstancy is the summons to individuation. We are neither our point of origin nor our goal; the former is long gone; the latter forever recedes as we move forward. We are the journey itself.[2]

-James Hollis, Swamplands of the Soul

[2] Swamplands of the Soul, p 51

FRED

Chapter one

The evening sun on the bedroom wall wakes Fred from his nap. His sleep has been restless, the days and nights folding into one another with a tiresome rhythm. From the kitchen comes the sound of murmuring voices. "How is he today?" "About the same, he sleeps most of the time." Fred wonders if he is hungry, for he has no appetite these days, and just at that moment his daughter appears in the doorway of the bedroom with his small bowl of soup. This soup has been his supper for as long as he remembers; little dumplings made from dough of flour and potatoes and boiled in milk. "A poor man's supper," he always called it, for a poor man is all he has ever been.

"How are you feeling, Dad?" She comes closer and Fred turns his head to watch her. "Do you need me to help you?" She smiles and sets the bowl on the table beside his bed. Fred raises himself up on his pillows and reaches for the bowl. With a spoon he picks out the dumplings and slowly savors each one, pressing them softly between his gums. When the dumplings are finished, he lifts the bowl and drinks the warm milk carefully, but still he feels it trickling down his chin and into the white wisps of his beard.

"Here Dad, let me help you with that." She gently wipes his beard with the cloth she has in her hand. "Is there anything else you need Dad?" He shakes his head slightly and she leans forward to smooth the sheet over his frail bones. When did I get so small, he wonders to himself? He sees his hands on the sheet, so thin, with the veins showing through the pale skin. He turns them over and sees the calluses that still harden his palm. He thinks of the plowing, the milking, the chopping; all the things these hands have done. Now they lay here on the sheets, so weak he can barely hold his bowl. Where did it all go?

"Can you come back later and read from the Bible?" She smiles and carries the bowl from the room, closing the door softly behind her. Fred moves carefully, turning to his side to ease the aching in his bones. By now it is nearly dark, summertime, and a breeze through the window lifts the curtains gently. There is nothing more to do but sleep. If she comes back to read the Bible, he will be sleeping. He will wake and sleep throughout the night, and all the next day. Nothing to do but sleep.

At midnight he wakes and moves again. He lies in the dark, silently, listening. He is alone, everyone has gone to bed. He never heard her read from the Bible and he feels an emptiness, for always, every night of his life, he read from the Bible. Before he could read, his mother read to him. "In this dark and sinful world, where else can we turn but to the Lord?" He has always reminded his family that there was no place else to turn. Where would we be without the Lord? Even now, thin, weak, old and in pain, he wonders, where would he be without the Lord?

From outside the window, out in the dark, perching on a fence post, or maybe the eaves of the wash house, a mockingbird begins to sing. For a while Fred lies in the dark, listening. Suddenly, in a moment, the gap of the years closes, and he is home. The Russian night is warm around him, the short summer when the night birds sang, surrounds him and he is young again.

While it is true that we can't go home again, it is also true that in a universe of exiles, when people's paths intersect, the journey itself may seem like a home, with the Other present for the while. No small thing.[3]

-James Hollis, Swamplands of the Soul

[3] Swamplands of the Soul, p 59

RUSSIA

Chapter two

Poor is all he ever knew. They were poor when he was born. They had been poor before, and now, more than ever, they were poor. Mom worked hard to make a living. She was a widow, what could she do? Sometimes he watched her sitting at night after working all day, and his heart ached with pain for her. She was a widow and Fred wondered if there could be anything worse—a widow, with no man to take care of her; no man to milk, chop or plow. Sometimes he worried that all the work would kill her, and they would be alone, he and his two sisters, Agnes and Susie.

In 1881 Fred was born, and before he was two years old, his mother was a widow. This was all he had ever known. Sometimes his mother talked of his brothers, Gerhard, Peter and Jacob. It was seldom that she mentioned them, for they had been taken from her when they were just boys, and her losses were so great that she never spoke of them. Sometimes at night Fred was sure he heard her sobbing, and always he felt a terror rising in him. If anything should happen to Mom, what would they do?

The people of the village were all poor, but most of the women had a man to look after them. Fred watched and wondered what it must be like to be a man. If I were a man, he thought, my family would never be hungry. I would take care of my mother and my sisters and no one would ever be afraid. In the way that boys have, he dreamed of protecting them. He imagined the cows that he would have, the way he would plow the fields, the wood that would be stacked for winter and the hens that would peck in the yard. By the time the long Russian winter arrived each year, there would be firewood, food stored, hay for his cows, and the barn would be repaired. In his dreams Fred was a man; strong, kind and hard working.

But Fred was a boy, a very small boy, and his mother was a widow. He remembered the days when she milked cows for the Jews to pay the rent. Early in the morning she left, no matter how cold or how dark it was. Winter in Russia is long and cold, but cows must be milked. The Jews were kind enough, and not even wealthy, like the noblemen who lived in the countryside, but this is how Mom paid the rent. Morning and evening she milked cows. Fred's sisters

Agnes and Susie planted the garden in the summer, hoeing and weeding in the hot sun. Fred often went with his mother and when he was yet only a toddler, she was teaching him to milk. "Just in case I get sick someday, and there is no one to milk the cows," she said as they walked to the barn behind the big house where the Jews lived.

One evening as they were walking home, he asked about his brothers. "Why did they leave, Mom, and why didn't they ever come home?"

And so, she told the story. "A man came from the South of Russia and took them away." They were little boys; seven, eight, maybe ten years old, Mom couldn't even remember, and even now, Mom could not remember why she let them go. "We were all so poor" she said, "and he told us that he would take the boys and we could follow later. We planned on going, we thought we would. But after Dad died and I was alone, I didn't even know how to get there. My boys are gone. I'll never see them again,"

She told Fred that her sons weren't the only ones that the man took. The people of the village were so poor, and he offered a chance at a better life. His name was Jacob Schartner. At the moment that they were leaving, the parents thought that they would soon follow. It was the only way they could bear to see their boys leave, but none of them ever followed, and their boys were lost to them forever.

Fred remembered the night that Jacob returned. Mom was still milking for the Jews and they had eaten their supper when there was a knock on the door. Mom paused and looked up from her weaving. She laid her head to one side to make sure it wasn't the wind, and when it came again, she got up and opened the door. It was cold, wintertime, and though it had snowed earlier, the night was bright with a full moon lighting everything like daytime. Fred followed her to the door and stood behind her, clutching her skirt in his small hands, waiting to see who was coming so late in the evening. There was a man standing there, tall and unfamiliar. Mom started to speak and suddenly he felt her start to sink to her knees. Who was this man who was making his mother afraid? In the moonlight Fred could see that he wore a military uniform and he had shiny yellow buttons all the way down the front of his jacket.

"Heinrich!" he heard his mother say, and the man stepped forward to catch her as she fell. "It's me, mother, Jacob," he said as he stepped through the doorway. Jacob? Was this his brother? Fred had only heard his name one or two times, but he knew that he was one of the three brothers who had gone away years ago.

Jacob lifted his mother to her feet and stepped through the doorway. He closed the door on the freezing cold night and stood there in the dim light of the lamp. Susannah and Agnes were standing, the sewing they had in their hands beside them at their feet. For a long moment no one spoke. Then mom began to wail, and it was a sound that Fred had never heard before. "Jacob," she sobbed, "my son, my son!"

"Mama, don't cry, please don't cry." Jacob helped his mother to her chair, gently smoothing her hair and taking her hands in his. "Where's father?" he asked, looking around the small room.

"Your father is dead, Jacob, he's been gone for almost three years. It's only me and Fred and Susanna and Agnes here now." Mom was shaking, her hands on his shoulders as he knelt on the floor in front of her.

Jacob turned his attention to Fred. "Is this a little brother?" He reached out to put his hand on Fred's head, looking him up and down. "My father is dead, and I have a brother? I waited too long! I'll never see my father! I should have come sooner, but I could never find a way!"

That night Jacob told them of his life so far away. He and his two brothers had grown up with another family, and after a time they almost forgot Heinrich and Leise and the two sisters they had left behind. The family who took them in had a large family of their own and had not planned on being responsible for three boys who were crying for home. As the years passed, Jacob, Peter and Gerhard began to forget that they had ever had other parents. They worked hard and so they grew to be men. Jacob had joined the Russian army, and Mom asked him if he understood that the Mennonites never served in the military; they would rather die than to pledge themselves to the government and be willing to go to war and kill. Jacob told them that there was not enough land or work for all the sons to make a living, so he joined the army, hoping to find a better life, and believing that maybe one day he would see his family again. Now his dream had come true, and he was nearby with his regiment and had been allowed enough time to make a short visit. He came to the village, not even knowing if the family was still living there, or if they were even alive. He had asked at a house on the edge of the village and had been given directions to his mother's house.

Fred never forgot that evening with his brother. There was something different about his mother that night. His mother was kind, and good, but not affectionate. She worked hard to support her family; she read the Bible and prayed with them at night, but there was not time for hugs or pats or playtime. The Mennonites in Russia were very poor. They were luckier than the serfs, who were nothing more than slaves who could be bought and sold, but even though the Mennonites, or Helpless Poles, as they came to be known, were not slaves, they were not actually landowners either. They had possession of the land for as long as they stayed on it, but if they should choose to leave, they would leave with nothing other than what they could carry with them. They lived in harsh conditions, enduring bitter Russian winters, and they made their living from the land.

But on this night, with Jacob sitting next to her, Mom was different. For the first time in his short life, Fred was unsure of her comforting presence. He had heard her weep, and it was a sound he would never forget. Now, as she sat next to her long-lost son, she seemed small and weak. Fred knew, even at such an early age, that she would always take care of him. His sisters were good, but it was his Mother who would never fail him. On this night she sat next to her son, holding his arm, from time to time stroking his head and finally, Fred fell asleep, listening to their voices as they pieced together the story of their lives since they had been parted.

The next morning when Fred awoke, Mom and Jacob were gone. He had gone with her to milk the cows, and when they returned there was black bread and coffee for breakfast. Jacob told them that he had to be leaving soon; he had only been given an overnight pass and he must return to his post. Fred looked at him, standing so tall and looking so important, and tried to make himself believe that this was a brother who had left so long ago. Fred wasn't sure he liked Jacob. He had made is mother cry, and he seemed strange and different. He didn't seem like a brother at all. Fred couldn't tell if Jacob liked him either; before he left, he picked the lad up and rubbed his head. He laughed and asked Fred why he had so many smallpox scars. Fred didn't know what that meant…he knew he had been sick, and Mom called it smallpox, but he didn't know that it left scars. There was not a mirror in their small house and Fred had never seen his own face.

Fred watched his mother's face as Jacob readied himself to leave. He heard her ask about Peter and

Gerhard, and did Jacob think they would ever come home? Fred was only four when Jacob came home, but it was something he never forgot. After that day, he felt less sure of his mother, not as confident that she was strong enough to take care of them. More and more he longed to be a man, grown and strong. He wanted to take care of her, and he never wanted to see her be sad again. Jacob walked away that morning after hugging them all goodbye, and that was the last time Fred's mother ever saw her son.

Time passed in the village. It was a sad place at times, as ten years earlier the biggest part of the village had departed for America. As the one hundred years of privileges granted by Catherine the Great came to an end, the Mennonites began to think about moving again. Their history was one of moving, always moving. They would give up any comfort, any wealth, any place that was called home, in order to be allowed the free exercise of their religious beliefs. Since the middle of the 1500's, when the Inquisition came to the Netherlands, they had been moving. Those who left gave up their land and any improvements they had made on it.

But Fred's parents decided not to go. The journey was a long one, and a frightening one. At the time it seemed simpler and surely just as safe to remain where they were. The village where they lived was nearly deserted after the departure of their friends. The school no longer had a teacher, the church was taken over by the new inhabitants of the village, and the Mennonites met in one another's homes for their services. They continued to sell their butter and cheese and woven linen, raise their crops, and take wood from the forest. They had livestock and planted their gardens. The Russian winters were long and cold, but the summers were good for raising crops.

After a time, Elizabeth was left a widow. She had three children, and they all worked hard. Mom still milked for the Jews and in the winter, she did her weaving. She walked for miles to collect the spun flax from the farmers and then she wove cloth for them on the loom that was crowded into a corner of their small house. When the cloth was finished, she folded it into a pack and placed it on her back and carried as much as she could in her arms. Off she went to deliver the finished goods, which were then sold in the markets and stores to wealthy people. Mother's linen was in high demand, as she could always be depended upon to do a flawless job and deliver at the appointed time.

Poverty and cold were the hardest things about life in Russia, but if you could get past the winter, life was easier in the summer. Aganetha went to work for a wealthy family and then it was just Susie, Fred and Elizabeth. With no man to make her living and do the everyday upkeep, Elizabeth was left to take care of nearly everything by herself. Fred was growing, and his dreams of being a strong kind man who took care of people and showed kindness to all who came near him never left him.

One summer day, when Susie and Fred had been tending the garden since early morning, Fred wandered off to the woods at the edge of the farm where they lived. The forest was cool and dark, and in the distance, he could hear the voices of the men who were cutting boards. Sometimes they would take food and go deep into the woods and stay for days. On this day Fred sat down with his back against the trunk of a tree and listened to the sounds of the birds calling, men working, and the wind rustling in the trees. Fred thought about the conversations that he had been overhearing among the men. By the middle of the 1880's there was already talk of unrest in the countryside. There were those who were talking of leaving and following their families to America. Uncle Abraham Schmidt, Mom's brother, had mentioned it to her, but she told him that she could never leave her sons behind. She still dreamed of being reunited with them and the thought of leaving and never having any chance of seeing them was more than she could bear.

Fred sat and thought about America. There were occasional letters from the family and friends who had gone. They said that in the beginning, life was hard, but that there were many opportunities, and if one was of a mind to work, one could purchase land, equipment and livestock and build a home and outbuildings before too long. Fred thought about such an opportunity. He knew that he would never go without his mother, but deep inside he dreamed of having such a life. Fred thought about his future. Poverty was hard. It was hard to see a future, and it was hard to make enough to stay alive. The winters were so long, and so cold, and if a man failed to work hard enough in the summer and store enough food, he ran the risk of his family starving to death come wintertime.

By and by Fred roused himself from his daydreams and started back to the edge of the forest. The sun was warm after the shade trees and Fred stopped and felt it on his face for a moment. As he started back to the garden where he had left Susie working, he paused; there was a man standing with her. Who could it be? Even from this distance, Fred knew that the man was a stranger. He went closer, curious to see who the visitor was. Just then Susie saw him and waved and called out to him. "Fred, come see who's here!" Fred came closer and the man began to walk towards him. "It's Gerhard!" cried Susannah. Gerhard! Could it be? Had another brother come to visit?

So, Gerhard had come home. He told them that he never felt at home in the place where they had been taken, and when he had seen Jacob, and Jacob told him that his mother was still in the same village, he made up his mind that one day he would return. Mom was milking that late afternoon, and they sat on the ground in the fading sun as it began to get dark, talking. Soon Mother came walking up from the barn and Gerhard rose up to go meet her. Fred watched her the way he had watched when Jacob came home. She paused for a moment when she saw him and then she rushed towards him. "It's my son," she cried, "but I don't even know which one!"

Fred watched her embrace him and call him by name. "Gerhard, Gerhard, you're back!" They sat in the garden as the sun went down and then they went inside to have their supper. In the summertime there was an abundance of garden vegetables, cabbages, cucumbers, potatoes and corn. That evening they sat up late, while Gerhard told them of his life. He told them that he had made up his mind to return home and see if it would be possible for him to come back and make his life with them. He promised he was going to stay, and they would never have to be apart again!

Gerhard, like Jacob, lamented that he had waited too long and had never been able to see his father again. Mom sat watching him, tears forming in her eyes and rolling down her lined cheeks. Oh, if only her son would come home, maybe life would be easier. Maybe he would help her, and she wouldn't be a widow with no man to help.

The days that followed were new and different for Fred. Gerhard proved to be a kind brother, and Fred loved to follow him around. Gerhard set about looking for a piece of property to purchase. He told them he wanted to get married and come back and build a house. He said he had his eye on a nice girl, and if she would have him, he would get her and bring her back and he would never leave again.

After most of the village had departed for America there were strangers who had moved in, but there were still parcels of land available to purchase. Gerhard found a small plot on the edge of the village, right up next to the forest. After negotiations with the owner, the land was purchased. Gerhard said he was ready to go back home and fetch his bride and they would return. He left early one morning, as chilly weather was beginning to set in. He told them he wanted to get married and make it back before the worst of the winter weather came. Mom said goodbye to him with tears in her eyes. Fred hadn't seen her weep very many times, and it always unsettled him. He hugged his brother and promised to take good care of Mom and Susie until he could make it back.

The days passed and soon it was winter. Mom was silent as she went about her work, but Fred knew that she was wondering if Gerhard would really return. Day after day they waited, and soon the winter snows came, and the terrible Russian winter had set in.

One day as Fred and Gerhard had been exploring the new piece of land, a small pig came out of the forest. Gerhard caught him and they carried him back home. They asked around, waiting to see if anyone had lost a pig. No one claimed him, so they had a pig. The rest of that summer and through the winter they fed him weeds. The Jew allowed mom to have slop and soon the little pig had grown fat.

When spring came Mom was still looking for Gerhard. One day a letter came. Mom opened it with shaking hands. Gerhard wrote that the girl he had married was not interested in coming with him and he had decided to stay where he was. He told mom that the land he had bought belonged to her and she could build a house on it and live there if she wanted to. He said he would send some money to help her purchase the materials and pay someone to help her with the building. Mom dropped the letter in her lap, her disappointment almost more than she could bear. To have him back and lose him again was worse than if he had never come.

Aganetha came home from time to time to visit, and the next time she came Mom told her that she wanted her to help her build the house. Aganetha decided to give up working for the family she had been with for years and come back home. Fred was still small, but he helped. Together they built a house. They found someone who was willing to come and build the oven, which was the most important part of the home. It was built into the center of the room and provided heat for cooking and for keeping warm. There was a little spot on top for Fred to sleep. No matter how the blizzards raged outside, inside they were as snug and warm as they could be.

Gerhard had sent enough money to pay for most of the house. There were people in the village who helped Mom and Aganetha with the building, and before long, Mom was able to say goodbye to the Jews and they moved into their new home. Without the rent to pay each month, and with Mom's weaving money, she thought she could surely make her own way. No more going out early in the cold winter mornings. Mom decided that during the warm summer months she would do as much weaving as she could, and before the weather got too cold to make the long trek to pick up spun flax, she would bring enough home to allow her to weave all winter long. Come summer time she would deliver the woven cloth and in this way they would make their living.

When Mom left the Jews, they gave her a little spotted hen. She carried it home and brought it into the house. She made a small nest in the corner, and through the winter the hen lived in the house. Fred loved the little hen and made her his pet. She laid an egg a day, and throughout the week they saved the egg, and on Sunday morning each one of them had a boiled egg. Life was much better, but the disappointment of Gerhard's failure to return had made Mom so sad. Fred always dreamed of helping to make her life easier. He dreamed of America, and once he even mentioned it to her. She replied that there was no way to go now, she couldn't possibly leave on her own, and since there was no one else ready to leave she couldn't make any plans. She was beginning to realize that perhaps they should make plans to move. Fred was growing and she understood that one day he would be of an age to be conscripted into the military. What a difficult position to be in! Fred was her only son now and the thought of him going to war and being forced to kill was more than she could bear. It seemed as though no matter which way she turned she faced an impossible choice.

The first winter in the new house passed and the family felt so safe and comfortable! Mom did her weaving, the little spotted hen continued to lay and soon she was sitting on a nest of eggs. The eggs hatched and mom chose three of them to grow into layers and the others were raised to make good chicken soup. The pig had been butchered and bacon and ham were laid by. By and by Mom was able to buy some livestock, and the family was able to provide their own milk, as well as some butter. They had enough to sell, and a little for their own use. It was Fred's job to milk the cow, and he remembered the days when he learned from his mother. He felt important, doing a man's work, and helping to provide for the family.

Spring was coming when suddenly Mom took sick. The weaving was not finished, and she began to worry. She took pride in delivering on time, and if the winter came to an end and the river was no longer frozen, she would have to take a long walk around to get to a place where she could easily cross. In the winter she liked to cross on the frozen river, as it made her journey almost a day shorter. There were wolves in the forests, and their howls pierced the freezing nights when the moon was full. Mom always tried to be safely inside by the time it was dark.

Eventually she was feeling better and was able to finish her weaving. She prepared to make her delivery, even though the days had been sunny, and she knew the ice might not hold if she decided to cross. Aganetha and Susie begged her to wait until the weather was warmer and it would be better to make the longer journey. Mom was stubborn sometimes—Fred had come to realize this. She went about packing up her goods and early the next morning she left, while it was still dark and cold. They knew it would be several days before she returned and they watched her go, praying for her safe journey.

Several days passed and they started looking for her to return. After five days they were beginning to feel the terror of families who know that their loved one is not coming back. Where was Mom? Even if she had taken the long way around, she should be back by now. The thought of her drowning in the freezing river, sinking beneath the surface never to be seen again, or being devoured by wolves haunted their minds. At night Fred slept on his warm shelf on top of the oven and in the morning when he woke, he looked at the place where Mom was supposed to be sleeping. Nothing! Where was she? Agnes and Susie went about their work with sad faces. Mom wasn't coming back. Why hadn't she listened to them?

Late in the afternoon on the seventh day they heard her at the door. They rushed towards her, grabbing her as she came into the room. "Thank God you're home!" the girls cried. Mom sank into her seat by her loom. She dropped her package of spun flax beside her and told her story. On her way to make her deliveries, when she got to the river, she thought it was frozen hard enough for her to cross. When she was close to the other side, suddenly she felt the ice cracking beneath her. She had just a short way to go before she reached the other bank, but suddenly the ice gave way and she was drowning in the icy water. She came up for air and grabbed for the ice in front of her, but every time she tried to get out, the ice broke away and she went down again. The water was so cold, and her hands were freezing. She could barely feel her fingers as she reached out again and again to pull herself from the icy river. She was determined to hold onto the pack that she carried on her back, but by now it was soaked with water and weighing her down. Over and over she reached for the ledge of ice in front of her and over and over it broke just as she was pulling herself out. Just when she knew that she had no more strength in her, as she was breathing one more prayer to God to help her out of the frozen river, she grabbed onto the edge of the ice one more time. This time it held. With all the strength left in her body she pulled herself out and made her way to the bank. The wind was blowing, and her clothes were soaked and clinging to her skin. She knew that there was a farmhouse some distance away and she managed to make her way to the door and beg to be let in.

Fortunately for her, the people who lived there were kind. They took her into their home and quickly gave her something warm to wear and hung her things to dry in front of the friendly Russian oven. They gave her food and let her stay for two days while she regained her strength. After a while the linen was dry, and her clothes were ready. She was warm again, and even though she dreaded heading out into the cold windy morning, she knew she must. She made the rest of her journey, exchanged her goods for more flax and started the long walk home. On her way back she took the long way around. She sat there in the late evening, recounting the story, exhausted and still shaking. What a horrible ordeal she had just endured!

LEAVING THE LAND OF THE CZARS

Chapter three

By the following spring there was talk once again of leaving for America. Mom seemed to have given up hope of having her sons near her and for the first time Fred began to see that she was considering leaving. When her brother Uncle Abraham brought it up, she began asking questions. How would they get the money to go, she wondered? How many wanted to leave? It was getting very difficult to leave the country and they began to fear that it might already be too late. What a sad life for a widow in such a poor condition! She had worked so hard and faced so many hardships. She was so devout in her love for God, and Fred knew that without God they would never have made it. If it was God's will for them to leave, surely, he would provide a way. Mom and Uncle Abraham and his wife prayed together, and when Fred was alone, he prayed. He began asking God to make a way. He knew that if they remained in

Russia, he would be required to join the military and the stories of the Russian army were making their way to the small village. It was not something that Fred wanted to be a part of.

Added to all the other difficulties that they were facing, the famine of 1891-1892 had begun to sweep across Russia. It is estimated that before it ended nearly 500,000 people had died of hunger. Times were hard enough already, but with the threat of famine hanging over them, there was a new urgency to their plans to leave.

The history of the Mennonites was one of moving in order to have religious freedom. They knew when they settled on the banks of the Volga River in Prussia that their stay was going to be limited. One hundred years is what they were promised. Now that time had been up for a while and those who remained in the village were faced with making a decision. The old preacher, Tobias Unruh spoke very discouragingly of making the move. He advised those who remained to stay and make the best of it. He told many dark stories of what would happen to them if they left. Fred wanted to tell him to be quiet; he didn't want to see Mom get discouraged. It seemed to Fred more and more that Mom was ready to go. His sisters were also beginning to speak of leaving. Life was so hard, and they were tired of the cold. They had heard that it was also cold in Kansas where many of the Mennonites had settled, but not like Russia. There were more frequent letters these days, reporting on the crops, the opportunities and the choices that were available to them in every area of life. Fred knew that he wanted to go to America, but he knew it was best not to push Mom too hard. She had a long history of making her own decisions and she would be the one to decide about this.

Uncle Abraham Schmidt and Peter Unruh began to send letters to America to inquire about the possibility of obtaining funds to make the journey. Soon a letter came from Tobias (Creek) Unruh and he told them he had mortgaged all his livestock and the tickets would be purchased. Many late nights of planning had resulted in a group of 17 who were committed to leaving.

By late October the preparations had been made, but there was also other news. Aganetha had married her young man, Peter W. Koehn. Mom was happy, because she had been afraid that Aganetha would decide to stay if Peter W. was not of a mind to go with them. The tickets had already been purchased, but Aganetha, always thrifty, had saved money from the little she earned, and she had enough for Peter's ticket. The wedding took place in their home, with the minister, Tobias Unruh officiating. There was sweet milk and wheat bread, and someone brought butter. The wedding was sad but exciting, as the small group knew that they would soon be parting from their friends. The journey ahead filled them with fear of the unknown, yet excitement.

Throughout the summer and fall of 1891 they sold their livestock and the possessions that they would be leaving behind. They had a little money, but they knew it would have to be spent very carefully. The tickets had been paid for but any other expenses on the trip would have to be paid for by those traveling. Mom sold the last of her weaving, and the small amount of money that she had laid by was carefully hoarded. Susie and Agnes also had a little money. Aganetha had enough to pay for her new husband's ticket, and he had a little as well, so after carefully counting and recounting, they were finally satisfied that they had enough. Now all that remained was to wait for the Jews who had been paid to lead them through the forest to safety. These men made their living helping people to escape to Germany, and they had given careful instructions.

The final preparations had been made and each person had a pack ready. They would only take with them what they could carry on their backs. Mom had saved linen cloth from her own weaving, and each of them carefully packed the things they wanted to take and arranged it so that it could be tied to their backs. Mom had her Bible and a few pieces of clothing. She looked through her things again and again, desperately trying to decide what she should take and what she should leave behind. She chose a few special items from her cupboard, and they all wore several layers of clothing. Fred had few possessions, so he didn't have any hard decisions to make.

On the night they were prepared to leave, the group assembled at the home of Elizabeth and her children, as it was closest to the forest. They left the house as though they had only stepped out and would be returning. There was a bowl of boiled potatoes on the table, as though they would be back to eat, along with a loaf of black bread. The group consisted of Peter W. and Aganetha Koehn, Abraham Schmidt and his wife and 5 children, Peter Unruh and his wife, Johann Schmidt and his wife, and Elizabeth Penner and her two youngest children, Susannah and Fred. They read from the Bible and all of them prayed, asking God for his protection and blessing on the journey. Fred looked around their small house one last time. He was sad to be leaving, and yet filled with excitement at what lay ahead. He would finally be able to do all the things he had always dreamed of. He could own property, he could own cows, he could plow, and plant and harvest and he could take care of his mother.

What a difficult and treacherous time it was! Fred thought to himself that it is hard enough to leave everything behind, but to not know for sure where you are going, or exactly how you will get there is another matter entirely. Many prayers went up, begging God for his providence and care.

The hour came when it was time to leave. The Jews had left a message at a prearranged place earlier in the day. They would make their way to the boundary and then there would be a dangerous trek to the Austrian border. The Jews had warned them that they must be very quiet, or it could end badly for all of them. Fred watched his mother when she heard how they would be leaving. She had written letters several months before, trying to contact her sons Gerhard, Peter and Jacob, but no reply came. How she grieved at the thought that she would never see them again. She left word with some of the people who remained in the village that she would send letters back giving information about how she could be reached, should her sons ever return looking for her.

After one last prayer and a tearful goodbye to those who had come to bid them off, the group of 18 people left their home and made their way into the forest. It wasn't long before they reached the border, and there they found the Jews waiting for them. In hushed voices the men told them that they must be very quiet; the children must not be allowed to make noise, and the guides would stay a distance ahead of them in case they were caught. Fred's heart was pounding, now that the long-awaited moment had arrived. He hadn't asked anyone what would happen to them if they were caught, but he knew it would not be good! He worried about Mom. She sometimes had trouble walking, and she had never gotten over the cough that had set in after the ordeal of falling in the icy river. Sometimes at night she woke Fred with her coughing, and he worried about what would happen to him if she should fall ill.

The Jews told them that they would give instructions on what way to go, and when the group caught up with them, they would give further instructions and then disappear until the group caught up. The way through these woods was dark and very difficult. There were wolves in the forest, and from time to time their howling was so close that Fred was sure they would all be eaten alive. There was marsh, mud and slime, and brambles that caught at their clothing. They were covered with mud and freezing cold by the time the guides appeared for the last time and informed them that they had crossed the border into Austria and now the children could scream as loud as they wanted to! They were safe!

The next task that they faced was making the way from Austria to Hamburg by train. The tickets would have to come from the money they carried with them. When it came time to board the train, they realized that they were going to be short if they bought a full fare ticket for everyone. Children 12 years and under could ride at half fare. Uncle Abraham Schmidt had five children and only two of them were under 12. His daughter Anna was 14, and Uncle Abraham decided that he would tell the ticket agent that she was 12, and he would save enough money by doing this to make sure they had enough later on.

With their tickets in hand they boarded the train. Fred looked around in amazement. In his short life he had never been away from their small village. He had never seen a train, much less ridden on one. The sound of the whistle and the rumble of the wheels on the tracks made him forget for the moment that many dangers were still ahead. He watched everything with the consuming interest of a young boy, wondering at the magic of it all.

When they were situated in their seats, the train began to lurch and pull away from the station. Fred watched his mother, and saw tears creeping down her cheeks. Leaving home, never to return! Oh, the prayers and tears that had brought them to this place. Had they seen any other way, they would never have left! But the spirit that had led their people for centuries still dwelt within their breasts. Move or be taken over by the world! They held their religious liberty above all else. They would rather give up their lives than their beliefs! These were the stories that Fred had heard from the time he could remember. His people were pilgrims and strangers, never at home in one place. They moved when God told them to go. The minister Tobias Unruh had told them many times how their people had always been ready to go when the cloud moved, and yet he had chosen to stay behind. Fred wondered what the future held for those who had chosen to stay.

The train was moving now, faster and faster. Fred had never felt such speed. It was amazing and terrifying at the same time. The conductor started his walk down the aisle, taking tickets. When he reached Uncle Abraham's family, he collected the tickets and then looked sharply at Anna. "How old are you?" "Twelve" her father replied. "No, she is fourteen," the conductor replied. "She cannot ride at half fare. Full fare or we will stop the train and she will have to get off." Anna began to weep, terrified of being left behind. Uncle Abraham turned to the rest of the group and said, "What shall we do, I don't have enough money to pay for a full ticket, they will make my girl get off the train!"

After some conversation it was decided that Aganetha would advance Uncle Abraham the money and when the group got to Hamburg, Uncle Abraham's oldest son Tobias would remain behind in Germany until they could send money from America for his passage. The full fare was paid for Anna and for the moment their fears were put to rest.

Uncle Abraham felt so bad! Had he only known how quickly the money would go, he would have made sure he had more. He had sold his few livestock and implements, but with a family of seven, his expense was greater than the others. Now he had put his son Tobias in a difficult position, but Tobias assured them that he was willing to stay behind. It was certainly a better solution than leaving poor Anna alone beside the tracks in the middle of the Austrian countryside!

The train clacked on through the night and the next day. By the morning of the third day they had arrived in Hamburg. Now Fred was in for another surprise! He had never seen such a city, or so many people. The train pulled into the station in Hamburg and they were only a short distance from where they were to board the ship. Fred was amazed once again at the sight of the ocean just beyond the shipyard. What other new things would he see before they reached their new home? It was almost too much for this little Dutch boy to take in. The world was certainly a more amazing place than he had ever imagined. Suddenly he felt like a stranger, lost among this sea of humanity. Where were the friendly faces and familiar voices? Now they had to find their way to the ships offices and see about their passage.

The group of 18 immigrants made their way through the streets, not even realizing their bedraggled state. The mud and briars still clung to their clothes, and they were beginning to be hungry. The food they had brought with them was gone and they had no idea when there would be more. All their worst fears seemed to be coming to pass.

At last they found themselves in front of the man in charge of their tickets to America, but there was more bad news! He informed them that their ship had already sailed, and they had been left behind. The members of the group looked at each other in despair. What now? What would they do? The man was very angry and spoke very roughly to them. No, he told them, it was not possible to sail on another ship. They would have to return home. But how would they do that? The little money they had was not enough to purchase train tickets for everyone in the group, and there was nothing waiting for them back home. Surely their venture had come to a sad end.

Uncle Abraham told them to wait and he would go back and talk to the man one more time. Peter Unruh went with him and they approached the man, who was dealing with other travelers. When he saw them standing close by, he turned on them angrily. "I told you that there is no way that you can travel, your ship has sailed and there is not another passenger ship with room for 18 more people."

Uncle Abraham began to beg and plead. "Surely there is something you can do for us, please, we beg you. We don't want to return home and we don't have any place to stay here in Hamburg. Please, in the name of God, have mercy on us. Please find another way for us to travel!"

The man told them to wait until he was finished with the people in front of him. Finally, he turned to them, still very angry. Uncle Abraham begged him again. "Please, I beg you, can you find another way for us to travel?" The man turned to walk away and told them he would be back shortly.

When he returned, he informed them that there was a freighter leaving in a few days, sailing to Baltimore, the S. S. Gothia, and if they didn't mind sailing on an old freighter, their tickets could be transferred, and they could leave with the ship. Everyone sighed with relief, and Uncle Abraham led them in a prayer of thanks. Now they could board the ship and continue their journey. What a relief! The freighter was old and not the best way to travel, they had been told, but it was the only way.

They knew that they would have to buy the food that they would need for the crossing. They were told to purchase bread, pickled herring, salted mutton, dried prunes and apples, and ale. They were told where to go to make the purchases and then to return and make sure they were ready to board the S. S. Gothia on time. There were still several days before they could board the ship, so they bought extra food, and found benches and seats where they could sleep while they waited for the ship to sail.

There was not a lot of money left, but they had been told the crossing would take 8 or 9 days, so they had carefully chosen their purchases, making sure they had more than necessary. When it was time to present the tickets to the ticket agent, they had yet another surprise. Peter W. presented the ticket that had been purchased for young Tobias. Once again, the travelers faced the rage of the man in charge. He informed them angrily that each person must travel on his own ticket. Young Tobias would have to use his own ticket, and Peter W. would have to stay behind. At this news, Aganetha began to weep, wringing her hands and sobbing. The thought of being parted from her new husband, leaving him behind in a strange city with no idea of how or when they would be reunited, was more than she could bear. So many difficulties were standing in their way. The lack of money caused so many difficulties. There was not time to find some work or send a message to America asking for more money. There was nothing to do but follow the instructions they had been given. With much weeping, Aganetha said goodbye to Peter and the group allowed themselves to be directed to the ship.

Fred turned and took one last look at his new brother-in-law, standing alone and looking after them. There had been so many surprises on this journey, so many disturbing changes of plans. Fred wondered if the older ones would have undertaken the journey if they had realized the difficulties they would face. There was nothing to do but move forward, pray, and ask God to keep them all.

When Fred saw the freighter they were boarding, his heart sank. It was a rough looking old ship, and Fred had heard the others say they would be traveling in steerage. He wasn't sure what "steerage" was, but he knew their accommodations would be poor. Little did he know how poor! They were led, along with a group of about 130 other passengers, to a door that opened to a set of steep stairs, little more than a ladder. Down below, the space was dark, and a suffocating odor drifted up. Fred helped his mother to make her way down the steps, holding her pack while she made her way down into the semi-darkness. What had they gotten themselves into? They were used to poor conditions, but this was the worst they had ever encountered.

When all the group had descended into what was actually the cargo hold of the ship, they had to pause for a few minutes to adjust to the dim lighting. Above their heads there were openings that let in a little light; other than those openings there was no other source of light. Ahead in the semi-darkness they could see rows of bunks lining the walls, two bunks wide and three high. They were instructed to choose their bunks and then someone would return later to let them know what they could expect for the rest of their time in this dreadful place. Fred heard the scurrying sounds of rats, and the smell had not gotten better, only worse, as they made their way closer to their quarters. How would they endure a week in this place?

By this time, it was the thirteenth of November. The accommodations were drafty and cold, and they had been told there would be no heat, only the blankets on the bunks to keep them warm. The canvas that covered the openings high above their heads would be left open in the daytime, unless it was raining or too cold. They were shown the toilet facilities, which were behind a wall, but there was no door. It would be the responsibility of the passengers to empty these receptacles daily, as well as doing any cleaning that might need to be done. There was one thing they were not warned about, but they learned it soon enough. Sea sickness was common, and there was no place to vomit but on the floors, or the bunk. How would they endure a week in such a place? It seemed to Fred that they had descended into hell, and for the first time he began to wonder if they had made the right decision by leaving home. At least at home they could be clean. The food was plain, but tasty. There were no rats, lice or fleas in their small home.

They were informed that during the day they could be on the upper deck, but often it was too cold and windy to endure such a dubious privilege. The choice they had was to remain below, gagging from the stench, or to huddle on the deck above, wrapped in a stinking blanket and trying to stay out of the wind. The ship rocked and rolled, and Fred learned what it was like to be seasick. Never in all his life had he felt so bad.

Added to this distress was the fact that Mom was coughing more. They had also been informed that if they were ill when they arrived in Baltimore, they would be rejected. Fred wasn't sure what it meant to be rejected, but he knew it would mean more parting and separation. Sometimes at night he offered his blanket to Mom and huddled, freezing, on his bunk. He had to drape the blanket over her after she had fallen asleep, otherwise when he tried to offer it to her, she refused him sharply. She was never afraid to let him know that she could take care of herself and was not in need of his assistance. Sometimes it hurt his feelings, but he knew that her burdens and responsibilities were great, and she could never allow herself to show weakness.

In the mornings, and again at night, the group of 17 immigrants gathered together to hear Uncle Abraham read from the Bible and lead them in prayer. They prayed before they ate their skimpy breakfast, and after they had eaten their equally skimpy supper. The food was going a little faster than they had thought it would, so they rationed it carefully. The bread was growing moldy, so they decided to eat it first and save the preserved foods for later.

They were also beginning to suspect the crossing would take longer than 8 or 9 days. The seas were rough, and terrible storms came in which rocked the ship and caused the openings to be covered with the canvas flaps. They were offered tea and some dreadful liquid that was supposed to be coffee, but they drank very little of it. As the days passed, they became more and more cautious about the food supply. They were already a week and a half into the crossing, and even though they hadn't had any word about when they could expect to arrive in Baltimore, they were beginning to suspect that it would not be soon.

The days passed. Cold, hunger and seasickness were ever present. It seemed that this journey would never end. Would they ever see America? Would they ever hear the kind friendly voices of their people who waited for them? Fred thought he had seen enough strangers to last the rest of his life. He was used to life in a small village, where everyone was familiar, and could be relied upon to be kind. He was used to a life where people helped each other, where they believed the same, ate the same food, and had the same past. He had not imagined that there were so many kinds of people in the world, and that so many of them could be cruel. It was true that they met many kind people as they traveled. Their fellow passengers in steerage were kind people, all of them suffering the same indignities and fears as the group of Mennonites, but when men spoke roughly or threatened the group, Fred resolved that he would never in his life hurt another person, especially someone who was in need.

After nearly three weeks on board the S. S. Gothia, they were told that they would be coming into the harbor in Baltimore the next day. They were advised to clean themselves up and were told that there would be warm water and basins provided, and they would be expected to form lines and take turns. They were advised that it would be a good idea to change out of the smelly and soiled clothes they were wearing, as it was advisable to present themselves in the best way possible when they left the ship. They were hungry, having eaten the last bit of food the night before. They would be half starved by the time they left the ship and boarded the train for Kansas on the last leg of the journey.

That night Fred slept very little. He could scarcely believe that their journey was nearing its end. It was now nearly a month since they had left their home in Russia. They had departed their home on November 2, boarded the S. S. Gothia on November 13, and they docked in Baltimore on December 3, 1891. Fred had encountered the swampy forest, angry Germans, cold, hunger, rats, fleas and lice, and sea sickness since he left his village. The travelers were weary, but excited. Soon they would see their new home.

Fred tried to imagine America. What would it be like? Would he have a friend? He had left one friend behind in the village, and he hoped for a new one. He was fond of Uncle Abraham's children, August and Heinrich, and he hoped they would still be able to be together once they reached Kansas. He had heard that often when the groups of immigrants arrived, they were scattered, as each family found their own property and set out to make their living. As long as he could stay with Mom, Fred knew he would be fine. He couldn't imagine ever being parted from her. He loved her, but even more than that, he worried about her. He worried about her health, he worried when he knew she was sad, even though she tried to hide it, and he worried when she had to work too hard. One day he would be a man, do a man's work, and he would take care of her. She would never have to worry again.

The ship docked the next day in Baltimore. Fred had never imagined he could be so happy to feel solid ground underneath his feet. He stayed close to Mom as they went through the necessary questions and examinations. Mom was able to control her coughing, much to Fred's relief, and nothing was said about separation. The next part of the trip was the last one. They would board the train for Canton, Kansas. Having been gone from home for over a month already, they were ready to rest. Fred could barely imagine a time when this horror would be over. They had known that leaving would be difficult, but it had been worse than they had envisioned, and yet God had protected them. Each time they thought there was no way out, He had made a way. For the rest of his life Fred would remember this time as the time when he learned, more than he ever had before, that God does not fail his people. In the years that followed, he told his children often of the hardships that he had endured, but how God had never failed him.

What an amazing experience for a young lad of twelve! Crossing the ocean and starting a new life in a strange country was certainly an opportunity to learn to trust God! After that, Fred was never uncertain again. No matter what happened in his life, he turned his eyes to God, knowing that everything would work out.

America! Finally, the travelers had set their feet on American soil. Now they were in for another surprise! The people in this new land were friendly and kind. The Mennonites were greeted with smiles and kind faces, but the people spoke English! In Baltimore, where they docked, there had been people who understood them, but now that they had boarded the train for the long trip to Kansas, they realized there was no easy way to make themselves understood. The government was encouraging people to immigrate, and the railroads wanted them to settle along what was known as railroad land, so they provided free travel by train once they arrived in this country. There was a little money left, and with this they purchased a little food for the rest of the journey. The train was clean and fairly warm. No more terrible smells, no more rats or fleas. Fred was pretty sure there was something crawling in his hair, but he hoped that as soon as they reached Kansas, he would be able to bathe himself properly!

It seemed that Mom's mood was improving also! Fred watched her as she began to take an interest in the landscape that flew past the windows of the train. They left the city of Baltimore and flew through open country, villages and farms. Aganetha was still sad. She worried about her husband. What if something terrible happened to him in Hamburg, and she never saw him again? The attitude of some of the people they had seen there did not give her cause to be optimistic, but Aganetha was stoic, as were most of the Mennonites. They had not endured centuries of persecution, opposition, hard work, poverty and relocating by being weak and faint of heart. Fred knew that Aganetha would find work, save her money and when Peter W. arrived, he would find her well and ready to get on with life.

All of it seemed so unreal. Fred wondered if he would ever feel at home in this strange new place. He had always dreamed of having his own livestock, of farming his own land, and having his own family. Would these dreams come true in America? Little did he imagine the hardships and difficulties that lay ahead. Fred would learn a valuable lesson; that we never escape trouble. The battle is never over, it just continues to change. No sooner do we overcome one difficulty than a new one presents itself!

After three days and two nights on the train, they arrived at Canton Kansas on the morning of the fourth day. Now the real trouble came! Up until this time, they had always known where they were going. They had always known what the next step was. Now here they were, in the train station, and no one spoke their language. They had no idea where they were going from here. They had arrived in a place of open space and few people, where no one spoke their language or understood them. They had been expected two weeks earlier, and the friends who waited for them had perhaps given up on them. They had no way to get word to them that they had arrived. What would happen to them if no one came? They had no money, they were out of food, and they spoke no English.

Mom showed no feelings. Fred couldn't tell if she was afraid or not. The men talked together among themselves, trying to decide what to do. Just then a man in a wagon came up in front of the station and saw the straggly group waiting on the platform. He began to speak to them. He told them that he spoke both German and Dutch. They asked him if he knew Creek Unruh, and he said "Yes, in fact I haul their cream. I saw them earlier today. They're expecting you. I'll let them know you're here!"

And so, the long journey was almost at an end. In only a short time they would be with friends and family. The weather was cold and there was a strong wind blowing, so they stayed inside the station, finding places to sit while they waited. The day passed and they began to wonder if the message had been conveyed, but about eleven o'clock they heard the arrival of wagons outside. Creek Unruh had come with two wagons to fetch them. Oh, how they rejoiced to see him. Fred had not been born when the first immigrants left Russia, but the older ones were overjoyed to see an old friend. Could it really be possible that they had arrived in their new home? Fred thought that he would never be worried again. If he could make that treacherous journey, surely, he could face anything.

Finally, everyone was in the wagons and they started out for Creek Unruh's house. Some of the group was going to Peter Unruh's home, so for the first time they were separated. As the wagons bounced and rumbled along, Fred found himself growing sleepy. It had been an adventuresome day.

When he woke, Mom was shaking him and telling him to wake up and get off the wagon. It was nearly midnight by this time, but there was a long table set with the most delicious looking food, however, much to the surprise of the Russians, there were dishes, and knives and forks. What did they know of such things? But Tobias was so kind, he instructed them how to eat. He explained that "In America, when there is more than one thing on the table, we do not fill up on one thing. We eat a little from all things." Yes, these Russians really did learn to eat in America! They learned to eat with forks and spoons, if you can imagine such a thing!

The travelers were so very exhausted, and they longed for a bed, but Tobias was not finished feeding them yet. He left the room and reappeared with a dishpan full of large red apples! After they had all had apples, they were put to bed in clean soft beds. What a wonderful restful night that was! Home! They were really home! In the morning Fred woke early. It had been a short night, but his excitement was so great that he could no longer stay in bed. He got up and saw that the men were already up and standing outside. He joined them and looked around in amazement. Tobias had an apple orchard and the apples had been gathered up and were lying in great piles under the trees. What an amazing sight. America truly was a place of abundance!

The next thing that remained was for these latecomers to make their own way. Each one of them had to find their own way to make it in this new land. Soon they were scattered, left to make it on their own.

It was six months before Peter W. Koehn arrived in America from Germany. Money was sent for him, but it is no surprise to find out that he was being defrauded and no one was telling him about the money. Apparently, the money was being stolen by the Germans and he was being used as free labor. After a time, this fact was uncovered, and after some communication with the young man, his ticket was purchased and at long last he was able join his young wife and the rest of his friends in America. There aren't any details about his time in Hamburg, and his crossing all alone, but one can imagine what a difficult time it was! More hardship and uncertainty!

Fred Penner wrote a lot of his memories so there is a fair amount of information regarding the life he and his mother found in America. He reports that after their arrival in America he and his mother stayed at Rev. T. A. Unruh's. (The name Tobias occurs over and over in the history of the Helpless Poles, and they are not all the same person. There are numerous men by the name of Tobias Unruh. The Rev. T. A. Unruh is not Creek Unruh). The next spring, he and his mother went along to Marion County with someone and Mother took on a job.

After a time, Peter W. came and took Fred to Lonetree, Kansas where he worked for some time for Andrew Nightingale.

"Here I became acquainted with Andrew's parents, Benjamin Nightingales. As a young boy these folks talked me into working for them for 6 years and they would set me up when of age just as if I were their own son. The promises were very good and were these—two good horses and a set of brand-new harness, a new wagon, new walking plow, a milk cow and one fat hog, so I decided to accept that offer. I spent my six years there and went through thick and thin and then after the 6 years I worked on the threshing machine and after the threshing season was over, I worked for Pete James.

Fred's dreams of being a man who worked hard had certainly come true! He was sad to be parted from his mother, but he was also glad to know that she was well taken care of. She was with friends, and they were kind people who cared for her. She still had to work, but not as hard as she had in Russia. Fred and his mother exchanged letters to keep up with each other, but from that time on, their times together grew less and less.

Then all at once George Harms came over and told me that he had found out about a farm or a half section which was for rent and he claimed it was too much for him alone, so we went down to see this man to see whether we could get this farm. This man told us we could have the farm, but he didn't want no bachelors on his place, one of us would have to get married. I kind of had this in mind already, so I told him if he would give me time till I would have my wheat sowed then I would see about it. He gladly did this, so we rented the farm. Now then it was required my farm tools, my horses and so on. The promise made by Benjamin Nightingale was about half fulfilled, I had to buy half of these things myself and go in debt about $400.00. Now then I went to work, never in my life will I forget what a poor start I had. I started on a 5-acre patch, it was a terrible hot day, there was sunflowers about 6 feet high, my plow was all rusty and wouldn't scour. I had 5 horses to the plow, one would pull forward and other backward, but I took it kind of patient and things started to go, so I plowed about 115 acres and sowed it in.

Now then the time was here when I would have to stick to my promise. Now in such a weighty situation a person does lots of thinking, but soon found out that God's ways were far different than mine. My mother and my two sisters, Agnes and Susie had such great confidence in Abraham Eck's girls. Mother told me how nice one of their girls could sew, and Oh! What a good cook she was, she could do everything, of course she said she isn't so very strong and when washday will come you will have to help her, above that, she is not such a wonderful nice looking girl, but you should think about yourself, by that she wanted to tell me that I was such a tough looking boy myself. And sure enough, they got me interested in Anna Eck.

Now the concern was how shall we make this thing go? Abraham Ecks lived in Oklahoma and we in Kansas. Here it happened there was a lady hanging around there by the name of Mrs. Lena Buller and she was just leaving for Oklahoma, so I and Mother decided to send word along with her and Oh! How that lady was tickled that she could be my spokesman, and after she was gone about one week, I received a letter from the Ecks that everything was OK and in unity. They told me what Sunday Preacher Henry Heer (that used to live at Longdale) would be at Fairview for a meeting and we could be married, so when that Sunday came, I went on the journey. Levi Unruh, one of my partners, came along, we took the train in Galva and the next day we came to Rusk at almost dark. As we did not know just where Ecks lived, we hired a livery rig.

Now here at Fairview a bunch of boys must have gotten wind of the situation, namely that one of the Eck girls was going to get married to a Kansas boy, so they sneaked around there every evening and looked through the windows to see this Kansas boy. When we drove in the yard it was all dark already and while we stopped and had a little talk with our driver, all at once Aunt Susie came thru the door with the dish water and heard us talk, she had in her mind that these were those window watchers again and she made a few remarks that I am sure if I had understood it, it would have been a terrible discouragement to me. It all turned out for the best and they invited us in, they lived in a sod house and had it whitewashed, and it was so light in there and everything looked so nice, Oh! We just had a happy evening.

The next morning me and Henry got up very early about 5 o'clock and drove to Isabella. There we left our team and took the train for Enid so as to get my marriage license. We stayed overnight at Uncle David Bullers and the next day we went home. Now everything was lined up and in order.

Now I want to tell you a little how people got married in olden times. When this particular Sunday morning came, Father Eck had an old-fashioned spring wagon. They covered the seats with some old blankets and hitched on an old team of horses that did not look any too nice. The parents sat in the front seat and we as groom and bride in the rear and off we went to church Those old horses were not in too big a hurry so off and on he poked them a little with his stick and said "now, now, run just a little bit again." Then those horses would try to trot a little again, but then we got to church alright.

Preacher Heer had a different way to marry people. We had to kneel down, and he laid his hands on me and prayed over us, we did not have to give each other the hand so then we were married. The whole congregation was invited for dinner, it was a very nice and bright day. So today, November 9, we have been married 50 years. I can uprightly say that these 50 years don't seem to me any longer than those 6 years that I had to work for those people, even though we had to go through thick and thin and many tribulations, so much sickness and many other discouragements. But above all we must say it has went well and we praise the Lord. The Lord has blest us both spiritually and naturally. God entrusted to us 10 children and they all live. To a certain time, they were all converted and baptized. Now our whole family counts 64 and 6 grandchildren are dead. Now our last wish and prayer is that we could all, parents and children and all our dear grandchildren, could meet above in heaven This will be our last wish and prayer till we finally close our eyes in death.

Fred and his new bride returned to Kansas after their marriage, but he tells that after a time his wife's parents wrote and told them that they thought it would be much better if they would move to Oklahoma.

We got us a big box car, we and Sam Koehns together and loaded all of our household goods and 7 horses in there, I myself went with the car and Mother with the baby went with Sam Koehns on the train, so we left our growing crop and moved to Oklahoma. When harvest came, I had to go back to Kansas and take care of my grain and ripe wheat crop, Mamma stayed with her folks and while I was in Kansas the next boy, Frank was born. So when I came back we had two boys instead of one. Then we farmed Lena Buller's place for 3 years, here John was born. Then we moved onto Frank Miller's place somewhat southwest of Fairview, here we experienced and awfully tough time...that house was so small and so terribly cold. The pasture only had a smooth wire fence, I couldn't keep my cattle in. There was no water, I had to haul water for the house use, the cows had a little in the creek but that soon disappeared. Then I dug a hole in the creek about 6 or 7 feet deep trying to get water for my stock. One Sunday when we came home from church the old bull stood in the well! I had to dig him out, that was a tough Sunday!

So, this is an account of Fred's adventures after he reached America. Fred became a preacher and I've heard it said that he never preached in English. The account above was translated by one of his daughters. Even though he escaped the terrible things that were coming to Russia, he still faced hardships in his new home, but surely, he never regretted his decision to immigrate.

He also relates that there were a few letters from his older brothers, but eventually they learned that all the family who had stayed behind died in labor camps in Siberia. Sometimes there is simply no choice, and we do what we must do. I can only imagine how his old mother grieved for the sons she had left behind, never to see them again. People who were brave enough to take on the task of settling the land in Oklahoma that was given away in the Land Run deserve respect! That is not an easy country to live in in any case, and it is difficult to imagine bringing forth crops from the hard red ground, or the sandy soil. The heat and cold, the wind and harsh weather conditions surely made it very discouraging. The Helpless Poles were not as helpless as one might first believe!

Anna Miller, the daughter of Elizabeth Penner's son Gerhard arrived in America in 1921. She had traveled to Germany to escape the war and famine that came to Russia after the departure of her family members. Her brother Jacob Penner arrived at Montezuma, Kansas several years before she did. The information that she gave tells us that all three of Elizabeth Penner's older sons and their families died in Siberia, after terrible suffering. Had Gerhard only returned to his mother's village when he promised, he most likely would have escaped the terrible things that were coming. Fred relates that both Gerhard and Jacob came back to the village to visit, but no other mention is ever made of their brother Peter.

Anna Miller left a long and detailed account of her life and she faced many, many hardships. There is no information available to me regarding her brother Jacob. But this is the story of the family of Heinrich and Elizabeth Penner leaving Russia and coming to America.

There is a lot to learn from Fred's account. From the moment of leaving their home near the forest in Poland, being led through the slime, mud and "what not" as he calls it, taking the train through Austria to Germany, until their arrival at the station in Canton

Kansas, there was nothing but uncertainty. On the train the fourteen-year-old girl is threatened with being thrown off. They were late getting to Hamburg and their ship had already sailed, and the stationmaster was very angry with them and spoke roughly.

I can imagine that they were a terrified group of weary travelers who watched this drama unfold, wondering if they would be sent back to Russia, and what all that might mean to them. Then they find out that Peter W. will have to remain in Hamburg. They find themselves on an old freighter on rough seas, with the trip taking much longer than they had first expected. Fred doesn't elaborate on some of these details, but we can imagine that those waiting for them in Kansas had been expecting them weeks earlier and when they didn't arrive, they were no doubt quite concerned. Their arrival at the station must have been quite a letdown. They had survived all the obstacles that were before them, and now here they were in a strange place, unable to speak the language, and with no idea of how to get to where they were supposed to be, but the last part of their journey finally came to an end and they found themselves well fed, even eating apples before bedtime.

It's sad that they all scattered after they arrived, but that was the way it went with most immigrants. After all the time of being so close, sharing the worries and fears of the journey, as well has having been close neighbors and family before leaving, they were now scattered in a new land. God had to be with them through all that they encountered and yet they eventually came to the end of their journey without any losses. We often take the hardships of our forefather's for granted, and it is worth our time to stop and ponder the sacrifices that they made so that we could have a better life.

And so we live, forever saying goodbye.
-Rainer Maria Rilke

EXILE

The triune dynamic of the quest is characterized by (a) leaving home, which means departing the old ego concept,
(b) enduring the enlargement of the consciousness through suffering, and
(c) achieving a new place of individual growth. It is also how a culture's vision is enlarged.

-James Hollis, Swamplands of the Soul

CULTURE

Chapter four

How do I tell the story of a journey that is inward? I can't rely on the telling of events when the story is about beliefs, although the events give a context for the beliefs. How can I tell of feelings and thoughts in words that will explain a crisis of culture and identity that is so difficult to live through that words can't even be found to explain it as it is happening? I have found that a combination of facts and feelings must be presented in order to make the story whole. And so, I begin with my story; events and facts intermingled with thoughts and feelings. The purpose is not to entertain, but to enlighten. So many people are struggling in a wilderness of fear and uncertainty. The way out of this place is a journey that requires courage and commitment, but there is no roadmap and the way is not marked.

In my life I've always loved simple things; the view through a window, a feeling of being at home, friends who stay forever. I've always feared change and tried desperately to hold onto things. Who knows, maybe it is some genetic memory of always leaving, always moving, and wanting things to stay the same.

I was so attached to my fondness for the past and my fixed vision of the future! It never occurred to me that I would have to give it up, and when the time came, I resisted doing so with everything in me. I marveled at stories of ancestors who left their homes and traveled to new lands. This is essentially the history of the Mennonite people—centuries of change and uncertainty.

Perhaps this is why I feared it so. Maybe I knew deep down inside that I was destined to be a wanderer, never to fit into the environment that I called home. When I heard a story about my great-great grandmother I was moved. I was amazed at her fortitude and bravery, while knowing that she had done something I could never do. I eventually did the same thing, only my journey was inward instead of being between continents and countries. The time came when I looked back to her example and understood her better, and I've always felt a kinship with this old Russian widow who left home and children for a better future. I always thought she made a very hard choice, but now I understand that maybe she didn't have a choice at all, and that she was simply doing the only thing there was to do.

How well I understand her now. We do what we do because of who we are, not because we want to do it.

I have come to accept a very unsettling truth. If you are deeply committed to a cause or belief, you will eventually be called to pay a price. It is deception to believe that you can believe in something with all your heart and never be put to the test. Sometimes people shroud their commitment in strict religious belief, telling themselves that they are committed because they are unbending. If you say you are willing, then you will be called upon to prove it. In spite of this, I find that people like to live on the safe side. They look for ways to give their all without the possibility of ever giving their all. This isn't to detract from their level of commitment, it is simply a statement about how difficult it is to foresee the outcome of complete commitment to a cause.

I was born into a strict religious sect. I was as happy as a child could be. There are many advantages to strict religious sects. They are safe, predictable and peaceful. My life was good. I never wanted a different life. Sometimes I wondered what it would be like to live like the outside world. Even though we did not live inside a walled compound, our life was the life of a village. There were strong family ties. We had a culture and a history that went back many hundreds of years. This is reassuring to a child. In a world where things were becoming more transient and uncertain, I loved the order of my life, and pitied the children who had not had the good fortune to be born among us.

However, it seems that unbeknownst to me, a streak of independence that was far stronger than one would have first suspected lurked with in me and it would eventually bring me to a fork in the road. At this fork, my people went on in the same direction that they had been traveling for centuries and I took another road. The details of what happened are perhaps a story for another time. It is enough to say that it was sudden, abrupt and horrifying when the time came. I was thirty-seven years old, the mother of three children, with a fourth on the way when my world fell apart overnight. It never entered my mind that I had been banished because people like me are dangerous.

Excommunication and shunning are not things that I would wish upon anyone. The pain of it is incomprehensible. People who leave by their own wish, for their own reasons, suffer a fair amount. To be cast aside involuntarily, for reasons that make no sense, is a horror beyond words. To be removed and cast out from your society and family leaves you struggling with your identity. In many cases, people never find it again.

Almost everyone living in North America comes from a family that immigrated at some point in time. Immigrating was difficult and involved many hardships. People left families and homes behind, in most cases never to see them again. The thing that is different about the Helpless Poles is that they had been doing this for centuries. They had a history and a religious background that bound them together and enabled them to keep a distinct identity regardless of how many countries they moved through or how many centuries passed. In this way they were different. From this group of people there evolved a sect of people whose lifestyle and belief system were unique. This imprint was in my brain and in my blood from the day I was born. I was told many stories and heard many things which reinforced all of this throughout my childhood. Now that I am grown and able to take a more objective look at things, I see that some things were misrepresented. They were viewed through the lens of religion and sentimental recollection rather than accurate historical information. Tales evolve that tell us what we want to believe. The truth doesn't have to be so much different, but just a little difference can change everything! Napoleon said that history is the tale that the victors tell!

I was raised in a group where love and acceptance relied upon behavior. Everything was conditional, and even though as a child I was never in danger of corporate shunning, I saw it all around me. I knew that if you made mistakes your life could be over, at least the only life you had ever known. Young people joined at an early age in order to be in step with their peers. If they had any questions, they quickly rationalized them away. Very few young people are strong enough or think deeply enough to put the questions to serious study. Such questions usually follow spiritual and emotional maturity. Therefore, if a young person became confused or discouraged, they just left and drifted away. The fact that many people never seek a meaningful relationship with God after they leave shows the extent to which they loved the church instead of God. They find impossible to separate the two.

With the church no longer in focus, there is no purpose in going through the motions of loving God. Because of this, young people either fall away and leave, or they stay and become more and more bound by the culture. They begin to be attached to the social life and the ways of the group. As a group, these people are very well off financially. They have their own economy, their own educational system, even their own fashion and are very much a closed society. Leaving presents too many problems, and all those problems are solved if one can only submerge one's questions and doubts and remain a part of the group. Who wants to remove their children from their little friends, cousins, grandparents and uncles and aunts? The parents themselves are terrified of negotiating unfamiliar terrain, let alone placing their children in such a position.

Because of this, they stay. Leaving will cost everything, and they become more frustrated with the boundaries, the rules and the legalism. They long for freedom, and yet they look at those who have gone on to make a new life. They see children who have fallen into difficulty, and other problems, which in their minds is a fate worse than death. They see parents who have encountered marriage difficulties. All these things have been predicted about those who leave. Those who are trapped fail to look around them and see the children of those who are faithful members and who have encountered even worse difficulties. Because there is a fear of punishment if marriage or family problems are revealed, there is seldom any help given to these people. Therefore, when a family is exposed to the real world, they have no capacity to handle family issues. Problems are still something that one conceals and denies.

People who leave and find another church are often drawn to non-denominational groups because of their loathing for tight knit groups and authoritarian leadership. They crave freedom and peace and fear judgment and rejection. Alas, the fact is that after years of being so tightly corralled, they are often unable to deal with freedom. Choices abound. Clothing, hairstyles, entertainment, social life and friends, marriage partners, education and electronic media, which had formerly been forbidden are now permitted. There is a fear and yet a fascination.

For fifteen years after my departure I struggled daily with the death of old dreams, beliefs, and inner identity. The fact that they were dying didn't mean that they were automatically replaced with something new. It only meant that I was left with nothing; there was a void that was more painful than the struggle. As I came to terms with what was happening and what was really the truth about my life, I was left adrift like a chunk of ice in the Artic Sea. The loneliness and sense of being disenfranchised was overwhelming. Added to this was the constant advice from loving observers that I really should move on and then of course there were those who insisted I really should go back. The juxtaposition of old and new, truth and untruth was deeply disorienting for me. I had no plan, no road map for the future.

But no matter what tsunami of fear and desperation was rolling over me, God has never failed me. In the end I suspect that was the lesson he was wanting to teach me. He wanted me to learn to hear his voice and to depend only on him, and the only way for that to happen was for him to remove everything else. When I was left with nothing but God, then and only then did I understand the extent to which I had relied on other things. That fact is the underlying theme of my story. We build so many structures in our lives to keep us safe and give us direction and they are only structures. Structures can fall, and ultimately will. Only God is forever and unchanging. I am now free; free to make mistakes, test new waters and chart my own path.

To many of the people in my old world I appear to be drifting alone in a sea of deception, but I wish they could understand that all of us must have the opportunity to learn and understand the voice of God for ourselves. It can't happen when there is an idea of

God standing in the way. He is so much more than I ever knew when I was trapped in an idea. The truth is so much more, and so much less. It is my hope that what I have learned will eventually be of use to others. I decided years ago that I would never waste a moment of pain and that everything that happened to me would be used in my life for a greater purpose.

EXILE

Chapter five

My interest in exile goes back many years. I have observed over and over how people leave home for what they think is a short time. They think they are leaving until things get better and they can go back. Sometimes people do return and resume their life at home, but then there are those who never go back. They find a new identity and a new way of life and eventually they realize that home no longer exists. At home, life has continued to go on without them, and to return and try to fit into the stream many years down the road simply isn't an option, for a variety of reasons.

I read several books by Sudanese refugees; young men who had been displaced by the civil war. I marveled at their capacity to go on with life and to establish themselves in a new country, especially after having been severely traumatized and most often orphaned. I tried to imagine starting my life over in a new country without one single relative, and in fact without knowing whether they were alive or what had happened to them. I have felt the same when I have watched movies about Holocaust survivors. To be the only surviving member of a family or town must be the loneliest thing in the world.

There is a movie called "All Star Refugees" about refugees from the civil war in Sierra Leone. They were in a refugee camp in Guinea. They had endured terrible trauma and to make themselves and the people around them happy, they formed a band. They had homemade instruments and wrote their own music. All of them had been severely traumatized by war. One man had only one hand. He told how the soldiers had come into his house and forced him to kill his own small son. When he had done it, they chopped off his hand. Others had lost all family members and their homes. The man who had lost his hand said that he simply believed that everything that happens in life is destiny and that he held no grudges. He said that if he were to return home and meet his tormentors on the street, he would "forgive and forget." He simply chose to believe that what had happened to him was destiny, and he held no grudges.

One day the time came when the war had been over for a while and various agencies began pressuring the refugees to repatriate and return to their homes in Freetown. The members of the band thought about it, but they were afraid to return, finding it too hard to believe that the war was over and that they would be safe. Eventually they decided, after a trip home to have a look, that they would go back. One man said "I have no option. It's too hard. I can't live in exile." Another one, however, the one who had his hand chopped off, said that he couldn't go. He said that he would never feel safe and that he would rather live in exile than to go home and face the danger.

Some early stories of exile are told in the Bible. Joseph was sent into exile, and in a most painful way; sold into slavery by his own brothers. They sold him instead of killing him when one brother begged for his life. He'd done nothing wrong, but he was certainly treated unjustly. What was he thinking as he traveled with the caravan? Was he thinking of ways to escape and return home?

In any case, we know that if he planned to escape, he was never able to do so. He found himself living in Egypt. At first, he may have dreamed of going home. Did he plan in the beginning to settle in and become an Egyptian? It's doubtful. He encountered many difficulties, and of course, looking back on his life now, we can see that they were a series of tests. Years passed. He was falsely accused and imprisoned. He was in favor and out of favor. He was completely alone. We don't know whether he made friends. The impression that is given is that he was alone. No doubt he became fluent in the language of the Egyptians. He observed and came to understand the culture. Eventually he was given a prestigious appointment. What had become of the dreams of going home? Had he forgotten his home? He married and had sons. Now he was even more tied to the land. He was politically involved and attached by marriage.

One day his family arrived, but Joseph never left Egypt until many years later, when his bones were carried back home by his descendants. Life in the strange land turned out to be permanent, and yet Joseph died knowing that it had been for a reason. As he said to his brothers, "But as for you, ye thought evil against me; but God meant it unto good, to bring to pass, as it is this day, to save much people alive." (Genesis 50:20) It made sense in the end, but in the meantime, Joseph had to live every day as though it was all wrong. He had to make the best of every day as it came.

Another story of exile is Esther. Her people had been taken from their homeland. She was not of the first generation to be taken captive, but she still remembered her home and her ways, through stories that were kept alive by her people. The daily life that they lived was still in a strange land, yet they lived day to day as though it was their home. One day the opportunity came for Esther to perform a service for her people and suddenly she understood that she was in the right place at the right time. Her uncle said to her, "Who knoweth whether thou art come to the kingdom for such a time as this?" (Esther 4:14)

Moses lived a life in the palace when he had been born to a very common family. A series of events caused him to be adopted by the king's daughter. The day came, however, when he felt a kinship with his people, and he killed a man who dared to strike one of them. This meant that he had to flee. He had to go into exile in a strange country in order to save his own life. He no doubt left without saying goodbye to anyone, leaving with no idea of when, or if, he would ever return. All that mattered was that he would save his life.

He found himself in a distant place, and there he settled in. His exile served the purpose that exile so often does—he was brought face to face with himself. Having been a haughty and arrogant young man, he was now humbled. Anything that might have contributed to his former position of honor had been stripped away. In the end it turned out that he was nothing but a killer on the run.

Did he dream of returning home the way refugees usually do? Surely, he dreamed of a day when it would be safe to go back home. Maybe loneliness overwhelmed him. Having been used to the life of being the king's adopted grandson, he had no doubt had the finest food and clothing. Surely there had been servants to carry out his every wish. Now he lived the life of a nomad in the desert. The food was most likely very plain, and it's probable that he lived in a tent. Exile is not fun or easy. He herded sheep for a living. Home…he must have dreamed of it often. He remembered the River Nile, the palm trees and the palace; how he must have longed for his home—not only the life of the palace, but also the feelings of kinship that had begun to develop with the Hebrew people, the people he belonged to by birth. Life in the desert was hard.

But something was happening to Moses. He was learning what refugees learn so often. Home is where you live. Home is where you are loved. He married a woman and had children. The desert was becoming home. If he were to return to Egypt now, he would be leaving another home behind. Nothing is as easy as it first seems. The life of the refugee is complicated. How do you sing in a strange land?

The years in the desert accomplished their task. He became smooth as a stone that has been washed in a river. Anger, pride, arrogance and impatience were all purged out of him. The hot desert sun and the relentless desert wind wore the rough edges off him and at the end of 40 years, God chose him to carry out an enormous task. We refer to Moses as the meekest man who ever lived. What seemed like a meaningless exile had a purpose all along.

The point is that Moses, Esther and Joseph had no idea that a purpose was being fulfilled. They simply lived their lives. Even though they no doubt dreamed of going home, the day came when home was with them. Everything changed. Repatriation was never an option.

Jesus himself was exiled from heaven. He was sent away, into a foreign land. Here he found himself among strange people, people who didn't appreciate him or know him. He ate their food, lived among them, tolerated their ways and eventually suffered a terrible death at their hands. Jesus was the first fruit. In him we have hope of the ultimate repatriation. We have the hope that exile can end. He was allowed to go home. However, suffering and sorrow became his lot in this life. He was the example we have that a life worth living will be a life of suffering.

Suffering involves forgiving and loving. Those who refuse to forgive and love will only suffer more. The only way to survive exile is to let life do its work; let the desert smooth the rough edges. Try to fight life and see what happens! Those who survive exile have learned that they must lay their heavy burden down. They must forgive, love and move on. They dream of home; they dream of returning. In their minds home is so beautiful, the food is familiar, and family and friends remain the same, but if that were so, they would not have left in the first place. Home is a memory. An exile never believes as he leaves home that he will never return. In the beginning, the idea of never returning home is too painful to bear. It can only be accepted day by day, year by year. Eventually home is replaced with a new life, and the challenge is to accept this new life and stop looking back.

Exile should serve a purpose. It is where we should learn to know ourselves. It should be where all device and self-deception are stripped away. We should be in the process of being prepared for a task. That task will always involve leading others out of the darkness. We can't choose what the end of our exile will be, but as those mentioned above who went into exile, we must live each day, extracting meaning and strength from every challenge that comes our way. When the time is right, and we are ready, the task will be presented.

War is the most common reason for exile. War sends people running from burning homes, from soldiers with machine guns, bombs and machetes. War makes madmen out of human beings. In every war there are the victims and the madmen. It makes no difference what race or culture is involved, the killers are madmen and they kill kind and decent people. War can be waged on many fronts. It isn't always bombs or guns that do the killing. Sometimes people go to war with a bible in their hand. Sometimes it is hearts that they kill. It's all the same in the end, as far as exile goes. Home is a memory and the road ahead has not been carved.

War is always accompanied by a multitude of losses. There is the loss of home, land, family and human rights. Sometimes people are maimed and injured in ways that never heal. Besides the fact of geographic displacement there is the inward displacement. How do you sing your song in a new land?

James Hollis, author and Jungian psychologist provides the paradigm for the journey that is inward:

Fear of further departure, fear of the unknown, fear of the challenge of largeness intimidates us back into our convenient rituals, conventional thinking, and familiar surroundings. To be recurrently intimidated by the task of life is a form of spiritual annihilation. On the other front, lethargy seduces us with sibilant whispers: kick back, chill out, numb out, take it easy for a while...sometimes for a long while, sometimes a spiritual oblivion. Yet the way forward threatens death—at the very least, the death of what has been familiar, the death of whomever we have been.[4]

In the pattern he describes, an outward journey of displacement is only the physical manifestation of the thing that happens to us inwardly. Those who are not afraid can undertake an inward journey that is every bit as daunting and disorienting as the one my great-great grandmother undertook in 1891. She left all that was familiar, and surely suffered the death of whomever she had been. Even though she carried her name, her experiences, her personality, her grief and her losses with her when she left her home, she was leaving the only context for those traits and characteristics that she had ever known. In her new

[4] Finding Meaning in the Second Half of Life, p 39

home, they resided within her, and no one looking on could ever see her as she really was. From henceforth she was seen as an old woman who couldn't speak the language and whose past experiences had never prepared her for the life that she lived at the end.

One can only imagine the sense of distress deep within her at the loss of her former framework. One must also assume that she never examined anything in any depth. The old was forever gone and the new was a strange landscape where she must simply reside until her time came to move on. And yet, because of what she did, today I live in a great land where I have never known war, hunger or fear of any kind. I can make choices, rise or fall because of them, and I will always reverence her memory. What a great lady!

Geographic displacement is not the profound issue in my life. I was displaced inwardly, and surely, I can fashion tools with which to carve a new path. No one can do it for me. Much as I would like to place the responsibility on another's shoulders, in the end it rests solely on mine.

Historically, the family evolved as an institution, including not only blood kin, but also all those who were present to carry on the work of survival, essential chores, and the transmission of tribal values. Gathered together, a group could better defend itself, differentiate roles and tasks, protect their young, and ensure their continuity.[5]

-James Hollis, Finding Meaning in the Second Half of Life

[5] Finding Meaning in the Second Half of Live, p 127

THE PERSECUTED

Chapter six

The exile of the Mennonites began in The Netherlands in the middle of the sixteenth century. Religious persecution began to drive these strict and devout people farther and farther from their homes, until they left Polish Russia in the late part of the 19th century and began the last leg of their trek, which brought them to North America.

The Mennonites were a group of people who were willing to give up everything, even their very lives, in order to live their beliefs. They suffered greatly, and many gave their lives. Over the course of centuries, they remained cohesive as a group. From time to time there were those who drifted away, often due to material wealth, but over the centuries, there was an intact group who moved forward, always driven by their strong beliefs and persecution.

I am descended from these people. In reading of their history, I see familiar names from 500 years ago; Jansen which became Johnson (my father's name) when they arrived in America, and Koehn, which was my mother's maiden name. I understand that it is unusual to have such a long and clearly understood genealogy. I can find the names of great-great-great grandparents (and in some cases further back) on both sides, and stories of their travels and hardships.

By 1521 in the Netherlands, Charles V of Spain had issued an edict and initiated the inquisition against all who would oppose the Catholic Church. Their writings were ordered to be burned and they were prohibited to meet. At this juncture they began to move and disperse. A timeline of their migration across Europe would show them moving, always moving. Because they were Dutch, they were skilled at repairing dikes and draining swamplands and this stood them in good stead as they found favor with kings and sought safety.

These people were known as the Anabaptists, and they were comprised of people who resisted infant baptism, the Mass, and confession to priests. A former Catholic priest by the name of Menno Simons was the catalyst that brought the struggling movement together, and whose name was eventually attached to his adherents. So, you can see that as a Mennonite, I can begin to mark my history at this point. It is a long and difficult history, and one that I have always been proud to own. These are people who did not bend or break, and who stood for what they believed in no matter what.

I won't go into a lengthy discussion of their beliefs and history but will dwell mostly on the journey over centuries through Europe.

The Mennonites began their migration through Europe in the late 1500's as they tried to escape persecution under the Spanish Inquisition. They moved as a group, and each time they relocated they would approach the king and ask for special favors. I have always envisioned a group of ragged peasants straggling off to visit the king! Most often they were successful in convincing the king to meet their demands. Following is a list of privileges granted by Catherine the Great when they came to Russia in 1763:

- *We grant to all foreigners coming to our Empire the unhindered and free practice of religion according to precepts and customs of their church.*
- *The settlers who have come to settle in Russian shall not be obliged to pay extra taxes to our treasure, nor to perform extra ordinary service.*

•*The settlers established in Russia shall not be liable against their will to any military or civil service.*

•*All lands allotted for settlement of colonies are to be given to them for eternal time, as an inalienable hereditary possession; not, however, as a personal property to anyone, but as the communal property of each colony.*

•*The colonists are permitted, in order to increase and improve their farms to buy areas of land from private individuals and indeed to acquire them as their property.*

•*The areas of land allocated by the Crown, as a rule, to be inherited by the youngest son*

•*If any of the foreigners who have settled here and have become subject to our rule should desire to depart again from our country, we will of course grant them freedom to do so at any time on conditions however, that they will be obliged to pay into our treasury a portion for the assets they have acquired in our Empire, after that, each one will be permitted to travel without hindrance, wherever he pleases.*

In 1786 the Empress expanded the list of benefits to include

- *Religious toleration.*
- *Military exemption.*
- *Free use of Crown's forests.*
- *175 acres of land for each family.*
- *Tax exemption for ten years. No Crown dues after that, only an annual fee of 7 ½ cents per acre.*
- *Free transportation to their new home.*
- *A loan of 250.00 to each family.*
- *Support for each individual at the rate of 5 cents per day til the first harvest.*
- *Complete control of their own churches and schools.*
- *A liberal degree of self-government.*
- *Religious propaganda, however, was forbidden among the native Russians.*

As the people moved across Europe, they made themselves valuable by draining swamplands and repairing dikes. Thus, when they came into a country, the king would often give them access to lands that were unusable, with the stipulation that they drain the swamps and make the land productive. This they did with great skill, and before long they were prosperous and thriving.

The Mennonites were invited to the Vistula River Valley in Polish-Prussia in the mid 1500's. They were successful in reclaiming vast wastelands and they came to the attention of the Crown. It was decided that the entire area should be settled by Dutch farmers. At this time, about 1568, there is a record of two Dutch farmers by the name of Peter and Thomas Jansen arriving with a contingent of other Dutch farmers. I like reading these accounts because I tell myself that these were ancestors of mine.

The lands were leased to these farmers but eventually they became the owners. The farmers were very successful in farming this land, but it flooded at least once every generation, which made a great deal of difficulty for them.

After a time, there were so many of these Dutch farmers that they were given special invitations from Dutch kings to come settle in the lowlands. Religious persecution had ceased, but nevertheless, they still faced opposition from the natives of these lands. The special privileges they were granted, along with their habit of remaining separate and maintaining their own language and religion, did not endear them to the original inhabitants.

As the years passed these people moved further into Poland. Frederick the Great was known for annexing vast areas of land and a good deal of it was too swampy for cultivation. Once again this provided an opportunity to move and spread out and once again, they were required to leave behind all property and land ownership. At this time, they were granted the following privileges:

- *Undisturbed religious liberty.*
- *Affirmation of yea, instead of giving an oath.*
- *Total exemption from military service.*
- *Their own schools manned with their own teachers.*
- *Sell their butter and cheese wherever they wanted to.*

It can be noted that during all this movement, no matter which country they were living in, they maintained their own culture. As long as they maintained their own schools and language, there was little opportunity for them to integrate into the culture of the country in which they were residing. It is easy to see that over the centuries the religion and culture only became stronger; they never weakened. They lived under strict religious convictions and have remained intact as a group for centuries.

Who has not felt insufficient to meet the demands of life, and wished for some deliverance? Who has not watched the familiar slip away and felt thrown back solely on one's own meager resources?[6]

-James Hollis, Swamplands of the Soul

[6] Swamplands of the Soul, p 53

SHUNNING

The only antidote to fear is to go through it. Only by embracing loneliness may its tyranny be broken.[7]

-James Hollis, Swamplands of the Soul

[7] Swamplands of the Soul, p 64

THE PERSECUTORS

Chapter Seven

People who have never experienced such a thing seem intrigued with the concept of shunning. No doubt there are degrees and types of shunning, but the kind that affects me is religious. In the world where I grew up, it is used as a tool to enforce the boundaries and to bring erring members to repentance. As I was growing up, I never questioned it. I was certain that it was a good thing and that if someone didn't like what was happening to them, they could simply repent and return. It seems harsh to me now when I think about it, but I had no idea what it really meant.

It is hard to know what makes people turn away from family and friends. I think I am incapable of it, but it is most likely just one of the things that I can't do. I am prone to other failures.

There are some psychological studies that cast a light on this phenomenon. In one, the psychologist Stanley Milgram conducted an experiment. He arranged a setting and procured participants. The participants were told they were helping him to understand how people learn. We know that rewards encourage good behavior, but he claimed that he was curious to find out what happened when people were punished for giving the wrong answers to a series of questions. Unknown to the participants, the "learner" was a confederate, a part of the experiment, and the true reason for the experiment was to see how far people would go in administering a painful shock to someone simply because an authority figure told them to do so.

The "teacher" (participant) sat on one side of a glass wall and the "learner" (confederate) sat on the other side. Through a microphone the teacher read a list of phrases or words, requiring the learner to repeat them in the proper order. In front of the teacher there was a console with a row of switches, each one designated as delivering an escalating electrical shock. With each subsequent incorrect response, the teacher was instructed to give a greater degree of electrical shock. At the far end of the scale, the label designated the shock as potentially fatal. As the teacher pulled the lever to deliver the shock, the learner screamed in pain and begged to be released from the experiment. As the shocks became more painful, the teacher turned to the white-coated authority figure who was sitting at a table making notes on a clipboard. "Do I have to go on?" he asks. Without looking up the instructor said, "It is essential that you continue," and the teacher reluctantly delivered another dose of electricity. Some of them asked who would be held responsible if the learner should actually die. The instructor replied that he would. The teacher sat there for a moment, looking uncertain and then delivered the shock. In reality, the learner was not receiving a shock, and his screams and pleas for mercy were pre-recorded.

A "shocking" 68% of the participants delivered what they believed to be a potentially fatal dose of electricity to the learner, simply because they were told to do so. They were reluctant to do so but they did it. The person they were trying to kill had done nothing to harm them. They had committed no atrocity; they had simply failed to remember a correct sequence of irrelevant words.

This reveals a rather unpleasant facet of human nature. When one believes that one will not be held accountable, one is willing to do a terrible thing to another human being, for almost no reason. The experiment was, of course, unethical according to the guidelines that must be followed today, and yet the truth that was revealed is unsettling. The teachers were carrying out the experiment one at a time. They were not participating in group behavior. They weren't looking around to see what others were doing. They based their behavior solely upon the instructions of a man who meant nothing to them and who was wearing a lab coat. Attire or a title that denotes authority carries with it a good deal of weight.

When considering the issue of religious shunning, this is quite revealing. It is next to impossible to convince one's mother or father or siblings that the punishment they are meting out is unfair or extreme. They look and speak like robots when they are confronted with the incongruity. They insist that the "church" requires it and they must do it. They insist that the culprit "deserves it." They claim that it is more painful for them and that it is a sign that they love you. All of this fails to offer much comfort to the one who is being tortured. Added to this is that the nature of the "crime" is about as senseless as the one in the experiment; the "learner" is simply failing to give the correct response which would reveal him or her as being compliant with the directives of the group, in many cases.

Another psychologist, Philip Zimbardo, conducted a study, also unethical by today's standards, in which he devised a mock prison setting. Half of the college students who were selected to participate were guards and the others were prisoners. Zimbardo wanted to see what would happen to otherwise normal and decent young people when they were put in charge of prisoners and left to treat them however they wished. Within a short time, the experiment spiraled out of control. The guards became so brutal, humiliating and abusing the prisoners so severely, that the experiment had to be called off after six days instead of the planned two weeks. Ishmael Beah, a former child solder from Sierra Leone, told me that he would like to believe that if he were confronted with violence at this point in his life, that after all the lessons he has learned, he would not respond with violence, but he has no way of knowing. He has already proven to himself that he can do things he would never have imagined.

It's a rather discouraging commentary on human nature to discover that we aren't nice, kind or good when faced with a set of circumstances. In the situation about which I'm writing, I was on the receiving end of the cruelty, so it is not my purpose to understand how cruel I can be. For my purposes, now, it is necessary to understand how I responded to cruelty. In the above-mentioned experiments, permanent discomfort followed the participants who had found themselves willing to kill, humiliate or degrade other human beings. In some cases, where participants knew one another (in similar experiments where participants were gathered from the same college dorm, for example) the relationships were never the same afterward.

When corporate abuse occurs, and one is trying to advance in one's degree of human development, a different approach is needed. Forgiveness is a word that means different things to different people. However, if one is to walk on in peace and maturity, forgiveness is required. Otherwise, the specter of the past continues to haunt, and hinder progress and growth. I found myself for years expressing to people what had been "done to me." This creates a position of victimhood in which the victimizer continues to have the upper hand. It takes strength, understanding and largeness of heart to leave it behind and deal with one's own issues instead of constantly berating those who have caused harm.

As James Hollis writes in *The Second Half of Life:*

> *Traditional cultures evolved communal rites to support a person's passage through such times and provided a vibrant set of mythological images that relocated the loss*

of the old in a larger, transcendent realm of meaning. In our era, however, such support, such rites of passage, are generally missing, or weakened, and these periods leave the individual adrift, disoriented, and alone. These multicultural rites of passage were always grounded in the transcendent images and sacred histories of the tribe; thus, one was told in so many words, "we do this, or understand this, or practice this, as first modeled and ordained by our gods and our ancestors, and our reenactment today mirrors and re-energizes their meaning paradigms for us. Compare that historic sense of the larger meaning of our natural deaths and rebirths with how today, when a person's personality deconstructs, he or she may be shamed, ridiculed, or pitied, and nearly always distanced, by friends and coworkers. For such isolated persons, the only supportive community may be found in the company of the therapist.

The most common characteristic of this kind of passage, despite the different story we each embody, is the deconstruction of "the false self"—the values and strategies we have derived from internalizing the dynamics and messages of our family and our culture. Yet, each person is invited to a new identity, new values, new attitudes toward the self and the world, which often stand in stark contrast to the life lived prior to this summons. In the absence of the tribe, the weekly ritual of analysis becomes the supportive rite of passage for some.

Although this transition from the old life and received values may prove frightening and disorienting, it is stunning, and ultimately transforming, to discover that something larger wishes to emerge. At this point in the journey, one is invited to experience deeper meaning in one's suffering, and to learn that something transcendent to the old way of being always comes when one has the courage to continue this journey through the dark wood. [8]

When I read this, it resonated inside of me. My personality deconstructed, and yet, far from having the tribe to support me, they were the ones who had cast me out. Not only did I have to find a way to go on, but first I had to find out where I was going. With all the past removed from me and the "transcendent images and sacred histories invalidated," my task was greatly intensified.

Some of us, understandably, do not wish to hear even this message of hope and personal growth. We wish to have our old world, our former assumptions, and stratagems, re-instituted as quickly as possible. We are desperate to hear; "Yes, your marriage can be restored to its pristine assumptions; yes, your depression can be magically removed without understanding why it has come; yes, your

---

[8] Finding Meaning in the Second Half of Life, p 28

old values and preferences still work." This understandable desire for what is called "the regressive restoration of the persona" merely papers over the growing crevice within, and off we go in search of another palliative treatment, or another less demanding view of our difficulties. It is quite natural to cling to the known world and fear the unknown. We all do—even as that crevice between the false self and the natural self grows ever greater within and the old attitudes more and more ineffectual. Most of us live our lives backing into our future, making the choices of each new moment from the data and agenda of the old-and then we wonder why repetitive patterns turn up in our lives. Our dilemma was best described in the nineteenth century by the Danish theologian Soren Kierkegaard when he noted in his journal the paradox that life must be remembered backward but lived forward. Is it not self-deluding then, to keep doing the same thing, but expecting different results? For those willing to stand in the heat of this transformational fire, the second half of life provides a shot at getting themselves back again. They might still fondly gaze at the old world, but they risk engaging a larger world, one more complex, less safe, more challenging, than the one that is already irresistibly hurtling toward them.[9]

It is easier to repatriate than to live in exile. I stood astride this widening crevice for some time,

[9] Finding Meaning in the Second Half of Life, p 31

desperately reaching back for the old while the new did indeed literally hurtle itself towards me. I resisted its approach and tried ever harder to make peace with what was receding farther from me. This discomfort can only be imagined. The worst part of it is that I didn't perceive it as a crevice that was widening; I simply thought that I was in a difficult position and if I could only restore the old ways of thinking and acting, the depression and the stress would be gone. Eventually, however, the breach could no longer be bridged. The old moved so far from me that I was no longer able to feel its foundation under my feet. I could fall into the gap and be destroyed, or I could move forward into the strange and unknown country that lay ahead of me.

It sounds easier than it was, and even at that, I know it sounds difficult. I saw nothing that I recognized in this new landscape. I gazed back yearningly to the old for a very long time. I didn't have currency to spend in this new country, I didn't speak the language, I had no tribe. To say I had difficulty does not even begin to explain what was happening. I wasn't aware of two continents drifting father apart. I only knew I lived with depression and sadness that were almost too much to bear. I fixated on my loneliness and my fear of the future. The framework of a village in which to raise my children no longer existed. To build a new one was unthinkable. I didn't want a new one; I cried for the old one like a child cries for a toy, even as I loathed and despised what had happened to me. Imagine the confusion for my children who were caught in this no man's land. They watched me crying for the old while telling them they must never go to it.

When one has lived within such clearly defined boundaries, their removal creates a fear and insecurity that is hard to describe. Before, I had felt like a drop of oil in a glass of water. Now I was just another drop of water, no longer distinct, no longer separate. I felt myself melting into the whole in a way that went against me. I grew up loving being separate and special. I grew up fearing the large ocean of humanity around me. I loved the safety of my walls. In loving them, I failed to see that they also constricted and smothered me. If I ever felt smothered, I consoled myself that smothering was a good thing, and it was the price I paid for safety.

I have said that it is easier to repatriate than to live in exile. If there had been a choice, I would have gone back. I would never have ventured on into that strange country before me if there had been any options. For 15 years I struggled daily with the death of old dreams, beliefs, and inner identity. During this time things were happening inside of me that I was unaware of. I came to a full understanding of my deep disdain for a system in which such difficulties were possible, in fact, even engineered and enforced.

As much as I longed for the old and a return to what seemed safe to me, I continually pushed myself on into new and more unfamiliar terrain. I have mentioned that I couldn't go back; I could have, but it would have required something I was incapable of. I would have had to be untrue to who I was. I was brought to the brink over and over, and no matter how much my life beckoned to me from across that divide, I had to say no. I would have died in some worse way if I had said yes.

To leave someone behind, to cast them out from their community and culture is a very inhumane thing to do. Those who do it to others have to be completely convinced by a hierarchy that what they are doing is the right thing, indeed, the only thing to do.

In the book of Numbers in the Bible, we read the story of Moses and his brother Aaron and his sister Miriam. Miriam had spoken against Moses and she was smitten with leprosy. The requirement of the law was that she be set outside the camp until she was declared clean. The multitude was ready to move on, but they waited until seven days had passed and Miriam could be readmitted. The entire company sat and waited seven days because it was unthinkable that they would move on and leave her behind. I continue to ponder what it must be like to be one of those who can banish someone without a second thought.

When you have suffered enough and stood as tall as these trees, then the snow will be a gift to you as a mantle of grace.[10]

-James Hollis, Swamplands of the Soul

[10] Swamplands of the Soul, p 136

HOME

Chapter eight

Life revolved around church when I was small. There was work, of course, and school for children, and just being at home, but church was the center of it all. When school ended in the spring, the next thing that happened, before we settled down to the endless hot and lazy days of summer, was Bible School. I write about this because when my mind goes back to it the memories and feelings are so strong.

The church was large, large enough to easily accommodate 500 people. The walls were painted a pastel color—sometimes pale green and sometimes pale pink. There were windows all along the sides with colored glass in them, some sort of swirly colors; not actually stained glass, but when the sun came through in the morning, there was a nice glowing effect that seemed very holy to me. There was a basement and a balcony, and it is in the basement that I most clearly recall my Bible School classes. First, we arranged upstairs in the sanctuary where the light through the colored windows was diffused on the pale pink walls. We had nice songs to sing—they still ring in my head when my mind goes back, and the superintendent would always give an object lesson which we craned our necks to see. Some children were bad, scuffling and whispering a bit, and the teachers would endeavor to keep order.

The basement was
cool. There were heavy burlap-like curtains that were pulled on wires to make classrooms. It was spring, or early summer, and flowers didn't grow easily in Western Kansas, but for some reason, my teachers always had roses. There was always a glass jar of colored roses on the table and I can still smell them. To this day when I smell roses, this is the memory that is aroused.

We had stories about Abraham and Noah and Moses, gummed stickers of animals that we pasted to a picture of an ark. Later, as we got older, the stories were about Paul and his missionary journeys. We had memory verses and they were printed on green cards. Each day we got a new one to memorize and they were strung together on a silver ring. I memorized the 23rd Psalm and the eleventh chapter of Hebrews. I loved memorizing. It made me feel as though I had done something worthwhile. The last day of Bible school, the tenth day, we stayed until late in the afternoon. On this day we packed a lunch in a brown paper bag and in the afternoon, we spent several hours practicing for a program.

Friday evening on the second week of Bible School there was a program. In a congregation of over 300 adults, nearly everyone turned out for the occasion. It didn't matter that summer was just getting underway and the women were tending gardens and butchering young chickens, and the men were busy harvesting wheat. The men parked their farm equipment early and the women made a simple supper so that there weren't a lot of dishes. The mothers had managed to sew new dresses for the little girls for the occasion. In spite of all the work my mother had, she always had a new dress ready for us for every special occasion. I remember her cutting and sewing and fitting it on me. She turned me around, checking from all sides. She plucked at the puffed sleeves to make them stand out and tied the sash in a perfect bow. She measured the hem, making the dress long enough to allow for my growth.

The program went on for a while. We filed up from the basement singing and took our seats in the front half of the church. Starting with the smallest children, each class took to the front of the church and performed a few songs and verses. The teacher mentioned how many students she had and how much money they had collected in the jar that sat on the table throughout. It was such a special time! I got to feel important. My small accomplishments were being honored by everyone, old and young. It was worth the trouble I had taken to learn the Psalms. "The earth is the Lord's and the fullness thereof, the world and all that dwell therein. For he hath founded it upon the seas and established it upon the floods..."

I'm telling all of this for a reason. It was such a lovely family life. Children were made to feel important. Their training and teaching were a priority. The parents, in fact, the whole church, turned out to admire their accomplishments. The feelings of being important are still profoundly imprinted on my mind to this day. There are a lot of complaints today about young people falling away from churches. This might be part of the reason.

It's possible they descend from a long line of church-going people, but church and family were not ingrained in them in this manner. In my world, the total interest that was taken in the children and their religious training was very secure and comforting. Children in other environments were possibly picked up by someone and taken to church while the parents slept or worked. Is it any wonder these children fall away from church when they become adults?

I was a happy child. My life at home was happy and going to church was an extension of the happiness and security that I enjoyed at home. Each one simply underscored and strengthened the other. There was no television in my life, no video games, and no recorded music of any kind. These things are not necessary for children to be happy. Today, if children don't have entertainment and constant stimulation, they become angry and restless. We played hide and seek, and other games. We roamed the pastures and the hay barn. There were animals to watch and chores to do.

Church was a regular part of every week; Sunday morning and Sunday evening, Wednesday evening in the winter, and occasions in between. Weddings were usually held on Sunday morning. Everyone was invited. The church was filled with people; the special hush was even more special than usual. People had new dresses and the women bustled busily in the basement getting the lunch ready. There was special singing and a sermon and then the bride and groom were married. The wedding lasted the rest of the afternoon. Funerals were also attended by all, not just by the family. The fact is that almost everyone in the church was a family. They were all pretty much tied together by blood or marriage, and most certainly by history and culture. The casket was carried out of the church by the pallbearers and taken some distance to the graveyard. We all followed behind and then in the cemetery there was more singing and some words by the preacher. In this cemetery lay the old bones of those who had come from Russia. There was a continuity and sense of the past that always overlapped the present.

All these occasions took place in a setting of love and familiarity. Neighbors and friends were the sum of my life. Never a stranger was to be seen. Comfort and security were all underscored by familiarity, and most of all, God. He sat watching over all of this, and he was very pleased. We loved the way we did things, and of course God did too.

In this manner we were quite separate from the world around us. We had a common background and culture. When I was young, there were still many of the older people who spoke Dutch and remembered the old ways. The old men had long white beards and the women parted their hair in the middle and tied a black kerchief under their chins. This was woven into my understanding of what it meant to be a Christian. There is nothing wrong with living a simple village life, but the problem arises when this begins to be understood as the way to be accepted by God. This part of my childhood story tells you about culture. Culture is important. Ethnic groups and nationalities have particular ways, languages, and religious patterns that bond them together.

There are rites of passage associated with strong cultural groups. We had them too. A child was expected to "join the church" at a certain age. For both boys and girls, this meant reaching the point where they knew the difference between right and wrong and they made a conscious choice to follow God. It meant that they repented of whatever sins a child might have, made confessions to parents, siblings, teachers, and classmates, and proclaimed that they were at peace with God. At this point (around twelve years of age) they were baptized and became church members.

This is all a good thing, but there is one problem with it: if a child has become a "Christian" at such an early age, and henceforth and forever believes that they have achieved the sum of the journey, it leaves little room for growth or experiencing any degree of true depth. It can happen of course, but to many people, this is the end of the journey and the rest of life is merely an extension of what was achieved at such an early age. From that point on, religion and culture take over. An alternate view would be that one starts early to make good choices, which will be of great value to them as they encounter ever larger difficulties throughout life.

Life at home was amazing, as I think back on it now. Simpler times are a memory for everyone my age, but especially for a little Mennonite girl growing up on a farm in Western Kansas in the 1960's. My parents worked hard to take care of us. I don't remember one lapse from my childhood that infringed upon my feelings of safety and security. I don't have one bad memory from my childhood. There might have been the occasional bad day or disappointment, but nothing that haunts me today and that I can point to and say, "That's why my life is a mess!"

Our house was old, but large and clean. My mother sewed, cooked, cleaned and canned for a family of eight children. I remember maybe two or three times in my life when she was sick and failed to be up cooking breakfast in the morning. I can truly say she never failed me! Of course, that's no surprise; she was the great-granddaughter of Elizabeth Penner and the granddaughter of Aganetha—women who built their own house and crossed oceans.

In the morning we all came downstairs and gathered in the living room. My father read from the Bible and we kneeled by our chairs to pray. My mother cooked breakfast every day of my life. I remember a couple of times when my father butchered a hog and the neighbors came to help. This involved a long day of making coils of link sausage and head cheese which were often included in our breakfast on winter mornings. The toast was always from bread that my mother had made. She made bread every single Saturday and it lasted the week. After breakfast we were off to school. When we came home my mother was always working. Most often she was at the sewing machine, because she sewed for herself and five daughters. She sewed every single dress I ever wore.

In the summer she hoed the garden, butchered chickens, canned fruits and vegetables and started sewing our dresses for school. My father worked from sunup to sundown. He was always kind and gentle, and I don't remember him being cruel or unfair to me one time in my life. There was never a drop of alcohol to be seen in our home, and I'm sure that neither of my parents had ever touched it. It never occurred to me that I would have any other kind of life. I loved my life with everything in m

When anything, even a good thing, becomes one-sided and excludes its opposite, the demonic enters in. Even goodness can be demonic when we are possessed by it. One thinks of Jung's concept of the shadow as the necessary dark side to every light; indeed, Jung noted, "more light means more night."[11]

-James Hollis, Swamplands of the Soul

[11] Swamplands of the Soul, p 67

A NEW HOME

Chapter nine

I was born into a religion that is more than a denomination. It is a culture and a closed society. It is a structure that incorporates every aspect of life. These people no longer live in villages where there is no intrusion of the outside world, nor do they live behind walls as some modern-day sects have been known to do, but they are still as intact as a group as though they lived inside a fortress. They own property that does not adjoin, as it did in the old days, they are free to come and go and live as they please, and yet, the walls around them, though invisible, are like those of a castle. The drawbridge is up over the moat and the turrets are manned.

Within this enclosure they are free to do as they please and they have a great sense of personal freedom. However, they are still inside the walls. The walls keep them in as much as they keep the world out. I left this world, not of my own desire or plan, but I left, nevertheless. I found for many years that I carried the walls with me. I was unable to go on with life or join the real world. It took years of anguished soul searching before I came to an understanding of freedom. The history of my ancestors and their unshakable faith, their willingness to leave everything and move on when their religious liberty was threatened, was a powerful force which bound me to the culture.

One day I was free of those walls and I moved out into the cosmic mainstream of humanity. At that time, I realized the extent to which I had been robbed. As human beings, we are a family. We have problems, weaknesses, and disasters, and yet, unless we can interact with our fellow travelers, we are being deprived of an essential human experience.

I would like to be able to report that I am fine, that I have resolved all my issues and come to terms with all my pain, but as of today, that is not the case. I have come to understand that some losses are too large to ever be completely resolved. Some wounds are so deep that they forever change the landscape of a life. The new one is unfamiliar and strewn with difficulty. The new life though, is one where the tools and understanding are available for navigating the terrain. Life is always new and changing, and strict sects try to stop the river of time. Life moves on, society evolves and what worked or was suitable a hundred years ago is aging and awkward in the 21st century.

This is not to say that God changes, but it is in fact his very quality of not changing that enables us to live in a world that no one had ever envisioned in past lifetimes. Technology and electronic media have created a strange world that frightens religious people. They try to sharpen their stone-age weapons into something that can combat the relentless challenges that threaten to destroy life as they have always known it and as they envision it for the future. It is my belief that it will never work. It makes something twisted and unnatural, and it produces spiritual dwarfs; those whose growth is stunted and whose vision is totally skewed.

God is available to meet every challenge. Forbidding and controlling will never be enough. Until a person or a society is strong enough to face whatever comes, they are not capable of living in this world. They will always be afraid, and they will always shrink back from challenges or change. It is a frightening journey out of the old world, but God will be there for anyone who is truly willing to grow. I have much to learn, but by examining the road I have already traveled, I hope that I and others can gain insight into the future.

The second half of life is a continuing dialectical encounter with divergent truths, truths that are generally quite difficult to bring to consciousness until we are forced to do so.

-James Hollis, Finding Meaning in the Second Half of Life

OF FOUNDERS AND RELIGION

Chapter ten

There is a movie based on a book by Karen Blixen (Isak Denisen, who wrote Out of Africa). It illustrates the power of religion to keep a lifestyle intact, but only until circumstances intervene. A person can have extremely high standards and proclaim loudly that there are things that they would never do. They can live a lifestyle that is based upon denying the baser impulses of the flesh, as they have determined them to be. Outwardly they seem to be very disciplined and orderly, but what is it that lies just beneath that strict and staid exterior? The same things that lurk in the breasts of all human beings!

The movie is called Babette's Feast. It is a tale of voluptuous sensuality set against the stark background of religious ascetism in a barren landscape. In the movie two sisters carry on their father's religious legacy after he passes away. Before he dies, both sisters have the opportunity for love but pass it by in favor of their religious life. Set on the windy rocky shores of Denmark, the movie shows the aging group of followers. They meet often in the home of the two sisters, where they eat meager portions of some sort of stew made from crumbled dark bread and ale. The sisters are do-ers of good deeds. The old men who live alone in their huts in the village wait each day for their bowl of gruel to be delivered. The sisters do their tasks with kindness and dedication!

One day a refugee arrives from the war in France. She's beautiful and sweet and she tells them only that she comes from Paris and is fleeing the war. She has been told that the good sisters will give her shelter. The sisters, Martine and Philipa, are sorry to tell her that they have no money for her wages, but she insists that she will live with them and work for free. All she wants is a safe place to live. In this manner she becomes their cook and maid. She learns to make the dreadful brown stew and they continue to hold meetings for the faithful in their small parlor.

The years pass. Babette maintains one tie to the past; she has left instructions with a friend in Paris to renew her lottery ticket each year. One day, after fifteen years or so have passed, a letter arrives for Babette. The sisters hover in the doorway of the kitchen waiting expectantly while Babette carefully washes her hands, dries them on a towel and slides her finger under the flap of the letter. She reads the note and holds up a check for 10,000 francs. The sisters are happy for her and yet saddened, because they are sure this means that Babette will be leaving them. They are planning a celebration for the small group of followers, marking the 100th anniversary of their dear father's birth. Never mind that the weekly meetings have begun to be marked with quarreling and strife. The long white beards and the stern black shawls mask hearts that are not as pure as they might appear to be. The faithful hold grudges, they repress anger and they are prone to arguing.

Babette tells the sisters that she would like to prepare the meal for the celebration. At first, they are hesitant to put her to the trouble, but she insists, and they give in. She warns them that she will be required to leave for a few days in order to fetch the supplies for the dinner. They explain that they had planned something simple; brown gruel, with perhaps coffee afterward, while they reminisced about the long dead minister. Babette smiles and departs for Paris.

Upon her return she requires men and carts to fetch her supplies from the small boat that brought her back. The sisters watch in horror. They see crates of wine, a large chunk of ice, a cage full of live quail, a huge live tortoise, crates and containers of crystal, silver candelabra, china plates and copper pots. They peep into the kitchen as she is unpacking the crates. "Surely that's not wine!" they say. She softly calls the wine by name as she fondles the bottle. The turtle waves his feet and makes snoring sounds from his place on the shelf. She speaks tenderly to the quail before she twists off their heads. "My little quails..."

That night in their beds the sisters dream of severed calves' heads and dancing flames. The next day the followers are brought together for a warning…Martine and Philipa deliver their message, clutching their brown cloaks around them tightly, with their fringed black shawls over their heads. They explain that they had no idea that Babette was going to prepare a Witch's Shabbat. At this point it seems that they would make the decision to refuse to participate in her plans, since a Witch's Shabbat would surely be seen as sinful, but strangely enough, nothing is said about withdrawing. However, they make the decision that they will eat her food and continue with the celebration, but that they will refuse to enjoy it. They won't even acknowledge that they are eating. "Not one word," they kept repeating. In other words, they agreed that they would participate in something that they saw as inherently sinful, but it wouldn't be a sin because they were going to make rules about how to feel about it.

The day of the celebration arrived. Babette had a red-haired young boy helping her to pluck the quail. An older whiskered man lent a hand, but Babette supervised the preparations. It so happened that the nephew of one of the women of the group had come for a visit. It was the first time he had visited the village in many years; in fact, on his last visit, he had courted one of the sisters and she had turned him down. By this time, he was a general in the

French army and rather sophisticated. The sisters warn Babette that there will be an extra guest, but she is not concerned. There will be plenty for all, she assures them.

The time comes for the dinner to be served. The table is draped with a beautifully pressed white cloth, set with beautiful place settings, silver and candles. As the old folks take their seats at the table, they whisper to one another to remember that they have lost their sense of taste. Babette sends the red-haired boy forth with the first bottle of wine, with instructions on how much to give each guest. The followers raise their glasses and through pursed lips they take a small taste. Their eyes show nothing; not a word is spoken. The general, who of course has no idea of the pact to keep silent, raises his glass in awe and declares that the amontillado is the finest he has ever tasted. The old ones lick their lips and try not to widen their eyes in amazement. One woman finishes hers with a slurp and looks around guiltily. She declares it to be some kind of lemonade, by way of explanation.

The various glasses continue to be filled. There is more wine, and champagne. The turtle soup appears to please them greatly, but no mention is made of it. The general spoons the broth into his mouth while seeming to swoon and declares it to be real turtle soup! The congregation remains silent, except for the sounds they make sucking their spoons.

The next course arrives. The general is almost weeping. He reports that in Paris there was only one place that served such a dish. This is most surely that dish. One chef, a woman, was known for creating this dish. It is a quail, plucked and apparently boned. Cailles en Sarcophage, we are told, was created by a chef in Paris, a woman who had the power to transform a dinner into a kind of love affair; a love affair that made no distinction between bodily appetite and spiritual appetite. She was considered to be the greatest culinary genius. Surely this is that chef! We were able to see Babette preparing the dish. She stuffed it with some sort of filling, and then sliced truffles and placed them tenderly on top of the stuffing before closing the breast of the bird, which was nesting in a bed of puff pastry. The tiny heads had been thoroughly cleaned and these she draped neatly over the edge of the puff pastry. When the general saw the dish that had been set before him, he sighed with rapture and took the small head in his fingers. Biting the head made a sharp crunching sound and the old people's eyes widened in horror as he sucked out the contents.

By this time, several glasses of very excellent wine into the meal, they were losing their resolve. The turtle soup had tested them greatly, but the Cailles en Sarcophage was beyond bearing. They could barely contain their pleasure as they forked small bites into their mouths. One old lady quoted sayings that the old minister had taught them. As she spoke, they all noisily gulped wine. The general turns to his aunt and says "a good meal Aunt," and she replies with a remark about the weather. He turned to another one of his dinner companions and commented on the food and wine. Once again, he was met with an observation about the weather, as the old ones continued with refusing to acknowledge any remark about the food. The wine continued to go down. They were silent but licked their lips and rolled their eyes in enjoyment.

When the red-haired boy came with another bottle, they held out their glasses to be filled. Their grim expressions had started to be replaced with smiles. Two old men who had a quarrel began to laugh and make up. One of them made a joking remark about how he had cheated the other and the one who had been cheated replied that he had known all along. The guilty party chuckled and said that it was even more than his victim knew, and the victim replied that he did in fact know. There was chuckling about this fact and the drinking of more wine. Clearly none of them had ever tasted wine before. Two old women who had been at odds began to reconcile. Martine and Philipa had long since lost their grim expressions and were eating and drinking happily. Each new dish that the kitchen boy delivered brought forth more exclamations from the general. He was in ecstasy.

These were the dishes that he had only experienced at the Café d Anglais in Paris, where the woman chef presided, and only she had the skill to do such things. No one paid him much attention…they were too busy pretending they didn't care about the food and wine, all the while licking their lips and asking for more.

The general decides to make a speech. He stands to his feet and repeats some of the statements that he memorized many years before when he visited them. He recites their favorite Bible verses and sounds very poetic.

He says these things while looking directly at the sister who had refused his attention years before. By this time, he understood what they were doing, and he understood also that each person makes a choice and they are content with that choice. Even though he had remembered their lost love with sorrow over the years, he now saw that he had been delivered from a fate worse than death; marriage to a very religious woman who had no idea how to take pleasure in simple things. And yet he held no grudge. He could love her now more freely than ever. "Everything is a gift," he said. The congregation listened to his religious sounding speech in silence, for he had quoted one of their favorite verses. Surely, he was profound, but they were not quite sure how. Religious jargon can sound very good but mean very little!

They ended the meal by eating figs and pineapple and finishing the wine. By now they were in very high spirits and laughter was beginning to break out here and there. They continued to reconcile and make peace with one another. "God bless you my dear…" "God bless you too, dear." The man and woman who had fretted about the unforgivable sin of adultery many years before shared a peaceful kiss. The general prepared to take his leave and said a sentimental goodbye to the sister he had loved so many years before. Does she understand what he is saying? She only lives with her body, while he has learned to live with his heart. He and Babette. Babette's pleasure was not in the eating but in the cooking of the meal. The general and Babette, the only two at the dinner who professed no religion were the only two who were honest and who were able to enjoy the gifts that they had been given.

When the diner was finally over, and the guests had gone, Martine and Philipa had a conversation with Babette. They told her they would be sorry to see her go. "Go?" she said in surprise. She has no place to go, there is no one waiting for her in Paris, and she has no money. No money? The sisters were bewildered. They ask about the 10,000 francs and she says she spent it all on the dinner. They are upset that she spent all she had on them and she says that it wasn't just for them, it was for her. She was able to make everyone happy when she gave her very best. She explains that the cry that goes out from the heart of every great artist is to be given the chance to do his very best. In alarmed voices they tell her that this not the end!

The candles burned down, and the snow fell outside the windows. Babette smiled sadly, understanding what they would never know, and that they would never live from their hearts, but only from their religious heads. She was the former chef of the Café 'd Anglais in Paris and she had asked only one thing of God—to be given one more chance to do her very best. This she had done when she prepared the dinner for the celebration, and if it cost her the entire fortune of 10,000 francs, she would do it with love. She gave all, and in so doing she gave abundantly—she emptied her heart for them. The religious ones had seen her offering as a sinful pleasure. Did they ever stop to think of what had been revealed? They had many strict beliefs. They had denied themselves of much, even love. It was true that there were some petty quarrels among them, but outwardly they looked perfect, according to their standards. The clothes were severe, the beards were long, and the hair was plain. They gathered often to sing about Jerusalem, their home. They remembered the late minister with reverence.

However, when the chance came to lower their guard, they did so. They thought it was alright because they were going to refuse to mention it. They surrounded the "sin" with rules that presumably made it alright! And yet when it was all said and done, they had participated in what they had believed to be a Witch's Shabbat, they had enjoyed it and they were different than before the dinner. Babette, who professed no religious beliefs or behavior, had shown more honesty and simple passion than they had ever felt. What is a sin?

Religion takes place in the head, spirituality in the heart. The fact remains that if you are controlled by rules and environment, you have not been put to the test. This exposes the difference between religion and true spirituality. In fact, I think one must be put to the test. It is only in the test that the truth is revealed. If you argue that even the country has laws, I reply that the ungodly, as well as the godly are controlled by these laws. In a religious society, where the people claim to know more of God than anyone else on earth, it is a different matter. It is those who punish the ones who break rules who are sinning. A person cannot claim to truly know God until there are no outward laws needed to control them. When the heart is fully converted, and the inner man has been fully tried is the only time that he can do away with all outward rules. Regarding the things of God, no one living human being can impose rules upon another and enforce them. The reason for this is that if the man has been fully tried, he will never want to enforce and punish and if he hasn't, then he doesn't know what he is capable of himself. All of us are capable of the same things, and a religious environment only masks this truth.

Babette was an exile who lived in a strange place. When she arrived in the village, she was sad because her husband and son had been shot. Her world no longer existed. She found a new way to live in a strange place, and the thing that made her special was carried within her, never to be lost. I love the way Babette sang her song in a strange land! When she had the opportunity to return home, she chose to stay in the new place, which by now had become home. She chose to give her most special gift to the people who had welcomed her. To be sure, they had their religious ways, but they welcomed Babette without questions, and they made her life in exile bearable. Religious people have many good qualities, but alas, far too often they lack the capacity to live from their hearts and to impart basic humanity to others.

There is a problem with religion; those who practice a religion are simply living from the template of someone who lived perhaps many hundreds of years before them. They are trying to embody the questions, fears and needs of someone who is long gone. The individual who founded the religion may have been expressing the dark side, or the shadow, as Jung called it, and those who try to replicate his beliefs and teachings are unknowingly living out the very darkness that troubled him; his guilt and fear and shame, or his need for power and control. What will it take for people to understand that they alone are responsible for their advancement as a human being, for how kind and caring and generous they are, and whether they leave the world a better place than they found it?

Without fail, religion crushes and suffocates people and prevents them from making their own honest mistakes and progress. Furthermore, when any kind of pleasure becomes sin, you can be sure that a twisted and perverse dynamic evolves. Guilt, shame and dishonesty are the inevitable result.

May what I do flow from me like a river, no forcing and no holding back, the way it is with children. Then, in these swelling and ebbing currents, these deepening tides moving out, returning, I will sing you as no one ever has, streaming through widening channels into the open sea.

-Rainer Maria Rilke

THE FASCISTS

Perhaps nothing which was ever real, which was ever important, which ever had gravity, is ever really lost. Only in letting go of the fantasy of control can one truly grieve loss, truly celebrate value.[12]

-James Hollis, Swamplands of the Soul

[12] Swamplands of the Soul, p 47

EVOLUTION OF A SYSTEM

Chapter eleven

An examination of the techniques used to keep a large group of people together and functioning as an identifiable body is quite interesting. These techniques have been distilled over thousands of years and used by many types of groups, whether religious, political or otherwise. Religious people like to dispute that any such dynamic is at work, but a closer look will reveal that it is more truth than not.

Families who have certain spiritual beliefs and belong to a strict religious organization practice a form of cognitive behavioral modification to keep the children inside the group and members under control. It is a system of punishment and reward. These techniques can become extremely distilled and ingrained over a long period of time. Add to all this the history of persecution, suffering and always being ready to move, as existed in the group I came from, and the dynamic is enhanced many times over.

One of the ways to control a group of people is to either hold out punishment for bad behavior, or reward for good behavior. In most cases the punishment and the reward are equally ingrained. Absence of the one automatically insures the presence of the other. Hell is presented as the consequence for the smallest infraction. All of this takes place outside the consciousness of the individual. If they were to be faced with this truth, they would vehemently deny it and attack and demonize anyone who brought such an idea to their attention.

A religion can become a social group. It can become very rigid, and it is strongly encouraged that the children do not leave the group. Imagine a religion that forbids you to leave. Imagine a religion that is so rigid and so distinct in how it developed that these ancient psychological manipulation tools evolved perfectly to keep people in place. Imagine adding to these factors the powerful ties of blood and history.

In a healthy environment, children are afforded the opportunity to express themselves and explore, which is ideal because the parent is helping the child to become independent. In a strict religion, the goal is dependence. The offspring may appear to be independent in many ways, but ultimately, their sense of identity is tied to the group and the fear of what will happen if they are disconnected is overwhelming. As James Hollis says in his book *Swamplands of the Soul:*

> *Every child, to become an adult, must sometimes transgress the parent's will. No parent can ultimately or always know what is right for any child, so the child must leave home, both literally and figuratively. Whereas in a healthy family, it is understood that the child must leave to become whole, in an unhealthy family (religion or culture), it is taught that to leave and find oneself away from the group is a transgression worthy of death.*[13]

We each need to carve out our own sense of identity. It is essential, and as we do it, we greatly test the patience and need of the parents for control. If a person has not been allowed to develop in this individual manner, they will lack the ability to regulate their own personality and have a stable personality. As a result, they become dependent on the personality of the hierarchy, or leadership of the group. Their identity becomes tied to the identity, or the history of the group. The opinion and approval of the hierarchy is sought for the smallest decisions and actions.

---

[13] Swamplands of the Soul, p 33

When you are this dependent, if your personality is so deeply tied to the dynamic of the group, when you are cut off, it essentially feels like death. In addition to this, remember that the hierarchy, or leadership has put a great deal of time and effort into replicating the personality of the founder of the group.

When you experience social ostracism or you feel like you're not being accepted, especially by someone you place a lot of value in, it creates a massive personality disturbance. If you are not embraced by your community, then you are just an outcast. You can completely lose your identity. If it is done to someone who is strong, they only get stronger. If it is done to someone who is weak, it can destroy them. It is a very dangerous game to play with the lives of other people.

If you are discouraged in childhood from having new experiences, you're not going to explore. If you're not exploring, you're not learning, encountering new information or the opportunities to solve problems. Your experiences and new material are only what is provided by the framework in which you exist. The boundaries are laid out and they must not be crossed. You are confined to a set of deeply ingrained ideas and a set of rigid individuals.

Anything outside of that framework that challenges the stability of that set of ideas is rendered invalid and is perceived as a threat. Sheep are created that cannot leave the pen. You are discouraged from exploration but are encouraged to accept and internalize the ideology of the group. This group has gained power in a variety of ways.

In the case of the religious group whose formation I am exploring, this power came about over centuries, as they faced difficulties, oppression, persecution, and as they overcame hardships and succeeded in every attempt they made to move forward. These qualities create an ingrained loyalty. The scenarios created for you if you leave are unbearable but on the other hand, the rewards for staying are tremendous. If one follows this dynamic out to its conclusion, one will see that such a group is full of spiritual infants; those who have never tested anything, never put their own beliefs to the test, never built their own foundation upon which to stand, and all because they wish to avoid suffering at any cost. And yet, these are the ones who boast of ancestors who suffered, went to the fire, the rack, had their heads chopped off, and were drowned…all because they would not bend or break from what they believed to be truth. Today their spiritual offspring cower at the thought of being socially ostracized. And is it any wonder? People fear being ostracized more than they fear having their heads chopped off, or so the conventional wisdom goes! Finally, the ultimate torture has been discovered!

We need stability, and part of the way that we get it is by internalizing certain beliefs about reality. Your beliefs are the building blocks with which you build the structure that is yourself. One of the things that happens in deeply traumatic experiences involving cruelty meted out by trusted and loved people within a group is that it makes you aware of the potential for evil within people.

If you've gone your whole life without experiencing it, and then someone you love and trust turns on you, it's a terrible betrayal. It can take a long time to come to terms with it. The disbelief can be very disorienting, and it threatens to bring down your entire structure. You will have to go through a period of questioning the potential of human beings to be evil and your own perceptions, or your ability to trust your own experience. One must come to accept that there can be evil behind the mask. To mask their own potential for malevolence, the group can present a picture of the outside world that is far more malevolent than it actually is.

At this point the individual's need for belief-stabilizing experiences is so strong that they are willing to accept almost any belief to keep their reality structure. They must build up a mystique of the powerful benign group, undergirded by the memories and history. They must make you believe that they are way more powerful than they are, and that the outside world is far more treacherous and dangerous than it actually is. Because we want to be accepted by the group, we will find ourselves believing things that are not true! We fear social ostracizing!

In the old days there was no need to build up a mystique; the movement was an organic thing, fueled by deep beliefs and the events surrounding them. Today the task is to sustain it when essentially the original fire has gone out. The group no longer lives under the conditions that created it, but they try to replicate the lifestyle and dynamic.

Excommunication from my church presumably takes place when one has committed a grave sin or has refused to be restored from what is diagnosed as a lukewarm or backslidden condition. I believed that this was always the case. I believed it was always fair and just and that it could never happen to someone unless they "deserved" it. However, all sects, no matter how well-intentioned they are in the beginning, are eventually forced to exercise certain measures in order to keep the boundaries secure.

When keeping the boundaries secure becomes more important than the hearts of human beings, a state known as "fascism" exists. In a fascist society, the whole is more important than the parts. The individuals must function with the idea that the good of the group is more important than the individual life. The dictionary defines fascism as a political philosophy, movement or regime that exalts nation and often race above the individual and that stands for a centralized autocratic government headed by a dictatorial leader, severe economic and social regimentation, and forcible suppression of opposition; a tendency toward, or actual exercise of strong autocratic or dictatorial control."

There are more factors involved in the political definition of fascism, but for the purposes of defining a rogue religious system, I will distill it down to a single definition: When human hearts are trampled so that the greater good can be achieved, I consider it to be a fascist religion.

All concepts, whether dogmas or operative beliefs, are husks which once held the energy, but which can also serve as a prison.

-James Hollis, Swamplands of the Soul

If we are limited to the capacities of our family of origin, our culture or our personal history, then we are truly passive sufferers of fate. If we can redefine ourselves, step into the abyss, walk across this imaginal extension of psyche, then we may more fully claim our lives. [14]

-James Hollis, Swamplands of the Soul

[14] Swamplands of the Soul, p 142

RETURN

Psalm 126

When the LORD turned again the captivity of Zion, we were like them that dream.
Then was our mouth filled with laughter, and our tongue with singing: then said they among the heathen, The LORD hath done great things for them.
The LORD hath done great things for us; whereof we are glad.
Turn again our captivity, O LORD, as the streams in the south.
They that sow in tears shall reap in joy. He that goeth forth and weepeth, bearing precious seed, shall doubtless come again with rejoicing, bringing his sheaves with him.

HOME

Chapter twelve

Sometimes it is possible, even good, for the exile to return home, but often it is not. It depends on what he has learned on his journey. Would a butterfly want to go back to being a worm? Would he want to fold his wings and forget how to fly? A great deal of it depends upon what has been learned on the journey. The question is not whether the road you have come up has been fun or easy, but whether you have learned anything.

Religious ideas are simple. They are not our own, but rather they are passed down from others. It is so very difficult to shed the skin that feels like it is a part of our very being and take on something new. The journey that I refer to is not always geographical. The transformational fire that James Hollis refers to is inward. It is the most painful and difficult, and yet the most rewarding thing we can do as human beings. The exile can return home, but it is often a new home! Our task is to find home wherever we are; to make the best life we can even when we are displaced. We must learn to sing in a strange land!

In reviewing the history of the Mennonite people, I notice some interesting things. They suffered persecution, and they were willing to die, suffer, or move for their beliefs. Religious freedom was the driving force among them. But imagine! The very things that were once done to them, they eventually did to others! In his book *The Helpless Poles,* Mennonite historian Abe J. Unruh states that the aim of the early Anabaptists was to "produce literally the primitive apostolic Church in its original purity and simplicity," and that even during times of bitter persecution, they found time to "argue over religious belief and human conduct." They were determined to present the Bride of Christ without spot or wrinkle. This is the trouble with religion; men policing other men, each one believing himself to be right, and in so doing they oppress and abuse. They believe that the only way to do this is to ban the members who do not conform to the standards of the group. When we argue over religious belief and human conduct, we have drifted away from the path!

Notice how little this has to do with a genuine transformation of the heart. Religious people, who obey the rules and conform to the standards of the group, can be some of the meanest people on earth. Menno Simons himself lived with a price on his head.

Those who would receive him into their homes, give him food or water, read his writings, or even speak to him faced loss of life or confiscation of property. And yet today, those who bear his name, Mennonite, will inflict these hardships on those who break with their traditions. They don't threaten loss of life or property, but they often forbid to read the writings of, or engage in relationships with, those who have fallen into what they would consider apostasy. The loss of life is not physical, but it can mean losing all that one has formerly held dear; relationships, a place at the table, fellowship and friendship. All for the sake of preserving a tradition!

It is true that we value the conviction and dedication of our forefathers. There was much good to be found there, but this business of religion will lead people astray every time. When protecting and promoting the organization becomes the primary concern, you can be sure that the truth has been lost. The truth is closer to what James Hollis teaches than what many religions teach. James Hollis states that "we must stand in that transformational fire!" What better way of saying exactly what Jesus taught? Let the difficulties of life change you! Become softer, kinder, more understanding and compassionate. Think less about yourself. Become generous, and helpful. Sometimes it is easier for people to be more like Menno, or some other religious figure than Jesus Christ himself!

I'm not only condemning the sect that I came out of; I mistrust all sects and religions. Sooner or later, every single time, they will deteriorate into an organization that is most interested in preserving itself; fascist, if you will. There are a multitude of good people within the ranks of these organizations, but even so, in the end, it becomes important for them to impose these systems on their children, and thus the system is perpetuated. The only way to preserve such a system is by instituting controls; some type of punishment for breaking the rules or leaving. Fear is the emotional vehicle used to transport the cargo of control. When I find that I am afraid of someone who tells me all about how they love God, I quietly retreat into the shadows. The Bible says that perfect love casts out all fear. Therefore, we can be sure that where fear exists, there is not perfect love. The example of Jesus Christ was perfect love!

One day our bones will be scattered over the earth and the details of how we believed will no longer matter. What legacy will we leave behind? Will we leave behind us those who learned something from us, those who were able to make it a little farther up the road by being with us, those whose hearts we touched with our genuine kindness? Or will we leave behind us the testimony that we rigidly adhered to the faith and upheld the rules of religious belief and human conduct?

Menno Simons is quoted as saying that "there is nothing I love more than the church." God spare me from the man whose first love is the church! He is bound to be mean. He is someone to be feared.

Abe J. Unruh tells how the Mennonites in Polish-Prussia faced difficulties because the natives of that area became jealous of their numbers and prosperity, and from time to time went to the king with requests that they be made to leave the land. He states that "they lived under continual fear of banishment." Today, those who transgress the rules of religious belief and human conduct face that same fear of banishment. The thing that the Mennonites once feared, they now carry out! Banishment! What a terrible word. No one wants to be banished! It strikes at the very core of our humanity!

To be clear, not all branches of Mennonites are the same. I am not naming the particular sect I came out of. It is not my intention to strike out at them, per se, from behind my pen. Rather, I want to encourage those who are in lonely exile, struggling in a wilderness of sadness and pain. I want to encourage them that sometimes suffering is a good thing. I have found, as I lost blood family and the support I supposed that I had and would always have, that God has provided a new family for me. There are those around me who love me, support me and give meaning to my life. That is not to say that I don't mourn the loss of my loved ones, but I have chosen to cherish the ones God has put in front of me. He has brought people to me who give my life meaning.

As I read Fred's story, I am always impressed by their unselfishness and the way they cooperated with one another. Creek Unruh was willing to mortgage his livestock to buy tickets. On the train, Aganetha was willing to part with her money so that Anna wasn't left behind. Young Tobias was willing to stay behind in Hamburg so that Peter W. could accompany his wife. When they reached America, there were a multitude of people who reached out and helped them. This has been the history of the Mennonite people; assisting, being compassionate, sharing their resources.

As for great-great grandmother, Elizabeth Penner, words fail me when I think of her courage and her suffering. Her life was a life of partings and loss. She was widowed before the age of 40. She lost many friends and relatives when the first group of Mennonites left for America in the 1870's. She lost her three oldest sons when they were just small boys, and eventually she gave up any chance of ever seeing them again. When she left for America, she left those dear friends and family who stayed behind.

I have always heard this story, and it was just the facts. Her boys were taken away when they were young. But what must it have been like for her to lose her sons? The stories that are passed down do not tell of her pain or her tears. I think of her working to take care of her other three children, milking cows in the cold in Russia. I think of her trekking miles to pick up spun flax and deliver woven goods. I think about her falling through the ice on a cold day and nearly drowning, then completing her journey and returning home. I think about her making the difficult decision to leave, and all the dangers she faced along the way. I think about her never having her own home again after that. She was 52 years old when she came to America and she died of stomach cancer at the age of 83. I wonder if she was at peace in her new home, or if she grieved and remembered the old days and what had been lost.

This kind of courage and fortitude humble me. I am so easily discouraged and so quick to feel sorry for myself. Living in a land of plenty can easily make us soft and entitled. I believe I must have all the things I want and desire. I can't imagine being cold and not having a way to get warm. I can't imagine eating the plain foods they ate and living the way they lived.

There is no doubt that an easy life draws us away from God. It is easy to make our religion a ritual, something that makes us feel good but that does not have much effect on those around us. In the memory of these hardy and determined people, I am committed to being kinder, more generous and more caring. Their story inspires me to realize that together we can make it!

Confronting each swampland as an implicit question-what is the meaning of my depression, to what is the anxiety linked in my history, what am I possessed by-allows us to be active instead of passive in our suffering. During this struggle we move from the fantasy of permanent happiness, or shame at not achieving it, to what is perhaps the greatest gift-the knowledge that we can live without happiness, but not without meaning.[15]

-James Hollis, Swamplands of the Soul

[15] Swamplands of the Soul, p 142

The one who plants trees, knowing he will never sit in their shade has at least started to understand the meaning of life.

-Rabindranath Tagore

LESSONS LEARNED FROM EXILE

Chapter thirteen

Those who go into exile often live a very long time before their purpose is revealed. Sometimes it is not revealed in their lifetime. Moses lived 40 years in the wilderness, believing that he was just passing the time until he died. Joseph was 17 when he was sold into Egypt. He was 30 when he was made overseer. He was 39 when his brothers first came to Egypt. There were a lot of hard years between the day he came to Egypt and the day his brothers arrived and he was able to do them a great service. My great-great grandmother died not having any idea of the full extent of the blessing that she brought to the lives of the many descendants who followed her. She may have always thought that she simply escaped war and famine and death in Siberia, but many thank her today for what she did.

It is easy for us to wonder sometimes if the sacrifices we make and the difficulties we go through are meaningful or have any value. I often think about my life and wish I could see more meaning in the things I have had to cope with. I would like to look back and see measurable progress. I would like to be able to say, "Aha, there was a purpose in this after all." I might be dead and gone, and because I never gave up, and I continued to try to shine a light into the darkness, someone who follows me will have a better life. I would like to think that I could have an influence just a little bit like that of my great-great grandmother. Sometimes we plant trees, knowing that we will never sit in their shade. Sometimes we learn lessons that we hope to pass on, but we may never live to see those who benefit from our struggle.

You might wonder what I have learned from my exile. In writing this book I have been brought face to face once again with the disconnection I have with my history. I read of the centuries of my people moving as a group, sharing persecution, poverty, uncertainty, but always together. When my path veered away from this history and went on in another direction, I became alienated from all that I had formerly held dear. Today, it is only me. I am alone. All this history, all of the family, all of the ties to the past have slipped away and I am alone. My husband has died, which might be why I was so saddened by Elizabeth Penner's state of being alone with no man to help out. All of my children have moved away. I have no family, not one single relative in the entire state that I live in. All the family traditions that I grew up with are no longer being carried out in my life. I could lament forever, mourning the loss of my own history and identity, but I have come to realize that God has mapped out a new path for me. He has given me purpose and meaning. He has allowed me to connect with people who are teaching me more and more every day about forgiveness, perseverance, strength and how to go on after all external supports have been removed. There were many times when I asked God why He didn't restore my former life to me and He simply answered, "You love it more than you love me." There is nothing more for me to say after that.

So, for those who fear exile and the journey towards something larger…yes, it will be painful. I can't promise you that you can hold on to the things you hold dear. But I can promise you that what you find will more than make up for what you leave behind!

Out there I see the world I missed and all the friends and family who've forgotten that I still breathe

-From the movie *Father Damien*

Bibliography

Hollis, James. *Swamplands of the Soul.* Toronto: Inner City Books, 1996.

Hollis, James. *Finding Meaning in the Second Half of Life (How to Finally Really Grow Up).* New York: Gotham Books, 2006

Unruh, Abe J. *The Helpless Poles.* 1973

ABOUT THE AUTHOR

Camilla Smith is a graduate of Mid-Continent University and obtained a master's degree from Lindsey Wilson School of Professional Counseling. She is a licensed therapist in private practice and the director of a non-profit organization, Tree of Hope.

The author may be contacted at fauxpoets@gmail.com

Made in the USA
Monee, IL
04 November 2026

67385507R10105